CONTENTS

MULTILATERAL DEVELOPMENT BANK PROCUREMENT

HEARING

BEFORE THE

SUBCOMMITTEE ON

INTERNATIONAL DEVELOPMENT, FINANCE, TRADE AND MONETARY POLICY

OF THE

COMMITTEE ON BANKING, FINANCE AND URBAN AFFAIRS

HOUSE OF REPRESENTATIVES

ONE HUNDRED THIRD CONGRESS

FIRST SESSION

NOVEMBER 18, 1993

Printed for the use of the Committee on Banking, Finance and Urban Affairs

Serial No. 103–102

U.S. GOVERNMENT PRINTING OFFICE

74–137 CC WASHINGTON : 1994

For sale by the U.S. Government Printing Office

Superintendent of Documents, Congressional Sales Office, Washington, DC 20402

ISBN 0-16-046359-9

HOUSE COMMITTEE ON BANKING, FINANCE AND URBAN AFFAIRS

HENRY B. GONZALEZ, Texas, *Chairman*

STEPHEN L. NEAL, North Carolina
JOHN J. LAFALCE, New York
BRUCE F. VENTO, Minnesota
CHARLES E. SCHUMER, New York
BARNEY FRANK, Massachusetts
PAUL E. KANJORSKI, Pennsylvania
JOSEPH P. KENNEDY II, Massachusetts
FLOYD H. FLAKE, New York
KWEISI MFUME, Maryland
MAXINE WATERS, California
LARRY LAROCCO, Idaho
BILL ORTON, Utah
JIM BACCHUS, Florida
HERBERT C. KLEIN, New Jersey
CAROLYN B. MALONEY, New York
PETER DEUTSCH, Florida
LUIS V. GUTIERREZ, Illinois
BOBBY L. RUSH, Illinois
LUCILLE ROYBAL-ALLARD, California
THOMAS M. BARRETT, Wisconsin
ELIZABETH FURSE, Oregon
NYDIA M. VELAZQUEZ, New York
ALBERT R. WYNN, Maryland
CLEO FIELDS, Louisiana
MELVIN WATT, North Carolina
MAURICE HINCHEY, New York
CALVIN M. DOOLEY, California
RON KLINK, Pennsylvania
ERIC FINGERHUT, Ohio

JAMES A. LEACH, Iowa
BILL MCCOLLUM, Florida
MARGE ROUKEMA, New Jersey
DOUG BEREUTER, Nebraska
THOMAS J. RIDGE, Pennsylvania
TOBY ROTH, Wisconsin
ALFRED A. (AL) MCCANDLESS, California
RICHARD H. BAKER, Louisiana
JIM NUSSLE, Iowa
CRAIG THOMAS, Wyoming
SAM JOHNSON, Texas
DEBORAH PRYCE, Ohio
JOHN LINDER, Georgia
JOE KNOLLENBERG, Michigan
RICK LAZIO, New York
ROD GRAMS, Minnesota
SPENCER BACHUS, Alabama
MIKE HUFFINGTON, California
MICHAEL CASTLE, Delaware
PETER KING, New York

BERNARD SANDERS, Vermont

SUBCOMMITTEE ON INTERNATIONAL DEVELOPMENT, FINANCE, TRADE AND MONETARY POLICY

BARNEY FRANK, Massachusetts, *Chairman*

STEPHEN L. NEAL, North Carolina
JOHN J. LAFALCE, New York
JOSEPH P. KENNEDY II, Massachusetts
MAXINE WATERS, California
LARRY LAROCCO, Idaho
BILL ORTON, Utah
JIM BACCHUS, Florida
HENRY B. GONZALEZ, Texas
PAUL E. KANJORSKI, Pennsylvania
BOBBY L. RUSH, Illinois
CLEO FIELDS, Louisiana
MELVIN WATT, North Carolina
ERIC FINGERHUT, Ohio

DOUG BEREUTER, Nebraska
ALFRED A. (AL) MCCANDLESS, California
BILL MCCOLLUM, Florida
MARGE ROUKEMA, New Jersey
SAM JOHNSON, Texas
MICHAEL HUFFINGTON, California
PETER KING, New York
RICHARD H. BAKER, Louisiana
JIM NUSSLE, Iowa
MICHAEL CASTLE, Delaware

BERNARD SANDERS, Vermont

MULTILATERAL DEVELOPMENT BANK PROCUREMENT

THURSDAY, NOVEMBER 18, 1993

HOUSE OF REPRESENTATIVES,
SUBCOMMITTEE ON INTERNATIONAL DEVELOPMENT,
FINANCE, TRADE AND MONETARY POLICY,
COMMITTEE ON BANKING, FINANCE AND URBAN AFFAIRS,
Washington, DC.

The subcommittee met, pursuant to notice, at 2:05 p.m., in room 2128, Rayburn House Office Building, Hon. Barney Frank [chairman of the subcommittee] presiding.

Present: Chairman Frank, Representatives Waters, Rush, Bereuter, McCandless, Huffington, and Nussle.

Chairman FRANK. The hearing will come to order.

We are here to discuss opportunities for involvement by American businesses in the work of the multilateral financial institutions. They have a major role in the activities of these institutions as do others.

We can't expect the multilateral financial institutions to act as if they were American institutions; they are multilateral, but we are of the opinion that insufficient attention has been given by almost all involved to exploring opportunities for American businesses to participate. Some other countries have probably been ahead of us in this regard.

So this is a hearing to begin the process of exploring what is going on and how we can improve opportunities for American businesses to participate.

Mr. Bereuter.

Mr. BEREUTER. Thank you, Mr. Chairman.

I am delighted you are holding these hearings addressing the subject of procurement and the MDBs. This has been a particular subject of interest to this Member for several years, one in which we have taken some action on several fronts in the last Congress as a result of the hearings earlier before this subcommittee.

I must commend the American Consulting Engineers Council who testified at that hearing and subsequently, at my request, drafted a number of recommendations for some effective reforms.

They worked with the Congress and later with TPCC to develop a more effective approach to procurement for American firms. Some of the legislative action that has already happened on this subject in the Jobs Through Export Act included improving the prospects for international exports.

One provision creates an additional full-time position for a procurement officer from the U.S. Department of Commerce under the

U.S. Executive Director of the World Bank and similar offices in each of the four regional Multilateral Development Banks for Latin America, Asia, Africa, and Europe. These officers help U.S. firms chase procurement opportunities in the $20 billion per year market of projects financed by these institutions in lesser developed parts of the world. We don't know what the track record is yet, but I have high expectations.

Another provision encourages more U.S. Government TDA funds be set aside to provide technical assistance trust funds so the MDBs can hire more U.S. professionals as additional consultants to participate in project design and appraisal teams.

This has been a particularly sharp need in the EBRD in their early startup stage, and we have felt the unfortunate consequences of not having these resources available, as do our European counterparts. The United States has had a very small program funded at a little less than $2 million annually, which has been successful in expanding procurement of goods and services. We need significant expansion of this program.

So, Mr. Chairman, I think the testimony today should let the Congress have a status report on implementation of these provisions. In addition, I have been pleased to see the TPCC report released on September 30, 1993 has identified facilitation of U.S. procurement in the MDBs as a priority. So let's continue to work together to tap this multibillion dollar MDB procurement market for U.S. companies.

Thank you for scheduling the hearing in a timely fashion.

[The prepared statement of Mr. Bereuter can be found in the appendix.]

Chairman FRANK. Thank you.

Our first witness is our colleague, Representative Traficant, who has a bill that deals actually with the Export-Import Bank, but it is relevant to the issue of procurement and of procuring a share of business for Americans overseas.

While we were going to have a hearing on the Export-Import Bank when this bill would have been more directly relevant, that hearing had to be rescheduled because of some conflicts. We are going to be dealing next year legislatively with issues with the Export-Import Bank and because there is a common thread—the degree to which we can encourage American businesses to become active overseas—we want to be involved.

There may be synergism between the two. So, Mr. Traficant, please go ahead.

STATEMENT OF HON. JAMES TRAFICANT, JR., A REPRESENTATIVE IN CONGRESS FROM THE STATE OF OHIO

Mr. TRAFICANT. Thank you.

I am honored to be here to present testimony. I have here a bill, H.R. 2192, that basically takes foreign aid in a little different direction. I have never been a great supporter of foreign aid.

We were talking about an awful lot of money and America's commitment to the newly formed Independent States, the former Soviet Union, and I had an idea. That idea was basically to help that economy with the making of small loans through joint ventures that would involve American small business entities and these loans made by the Export-Import Bank would help, through American small business enterprise, help that market economy grow by creating a presence of market oriented types of businesses within these newly formed States.

As this bill has started to circulate, it has received quite a bit of support. I was asked to look at how it could be applied not just to newly Independent States but in fact as a general program it could be guaranteed through the Export-Import Bank to effect some of these goals.

My bill that is being modified would start out with the newly Independent States and Africa. Here is how it would work. Up to $100,000 would be made in joint ventures to these particular entrepreneurs for opportunity for commerce and business in the Independent States and Africa. They would have to be in joint ventures with small business American firms with preferences that would be given for certain specifics. The maximum amount of the loan is $100,000.

Second of all, that this loan repayment would not be made on principal until after the third year and no interest accrued until after the fifth year and it would be set by a formula relative to the Consumer Price Index. The bottom line is it would not take a whole lot of money.

We ask for $100 million. The question is where do we get the money from. I leave that open and would ask for the advice, counsel, and support of the subcommittee and the chairman who knows best about this to determine the mechanism by which the program shall be funded, be it additional funds, newly appropriated from existing money.

The bottom line is by establishing these joint ventures, through these loans of the Export-Import Bank, the banks shall use the following criteria in making such loans. Preference shall be given to joint ventures involving small businesses located in economically depressed communities of our own country.

Preference shall be given to loans that will be naturally cost effective. Preference shall be given to joint ventures, naturally with the greatest likelihood of success to be determined by the bank.

Preference shall be given to joint ventures that are most likely to benefit the participating U.S. entities so involved.

Let me say one other thing. As this program could in fact be developed, there is some question of will some of these businesses in America seeing an opportunity maybe export some jobs over there. The bill in fact negates that and also negates any imports from these newly created and funded joint ventures and the products of those joint ventures.

The limitation on the amount of the loan is $100,000. As I said, the principal shall not be required until after the first 3 years of the loan and interest payments shall not accrue during the first 5 years of the loan and the rate of interest shall be based on the average of the Consumer Price Index.

I think this, for us just to continue to give money away is not necessarily helping those countries, and certainly not our own. I see this as a way of getting our business people two things; giving them a shot to make a dollar and to help the technical expertise and advice of our small businesses with the opportunity to make some money, also to help to give advice to these entrepreneurs in these two particular countries. I think that the program on the merit makes a lot of sense.

I would like to ask unanimous consent that my total statement be put in the record.

Chairman FRANK. Without objection.

Mr. TRAFICANT. The major thing is, Mr. Chairman, we are not giving away money. We will lend the money.

We are not lending a ton of money. They are basically smaller amounts and basically to effect small market oriented types of commerce activities in the Independent States and in Africa in concert with joint venture programs of our own small businesses.

With the preference I have given, it would fall within the scrutiny of your jurisdiction. I believe that there are a lot of our small businesses trapped in economically depressed communities that could also use a bit of a marketplace expander and this could be that.

I think the Export-Import Bank is the place for it to be and I think that it can be managed and it can be evaluated. My proposal is that it be limited, investigated, reported back to and moved from there, but I think the joint venture activity right now between Export-Import Bank and SBA is something like $1.3 million in total exposure, not a whole lot of money.

So as you could see this would not necessarily involve a lot of money. We have asked for $100 million and are saying whatever the funding mechanism you think best to effect the program, fine. You develop that.

With a number of the smaller deals it creates more opportunity, more diversity, more individuals involved, and more of an approach to impacting the economy with our market oriented type of system that will be good for both.

That is basically the thrust of the program. I think that it can work and I am asking you for help. I think it is a good idea, an excellent idea, and it is going to need some refinement.

The bill that is before you does not include Africa. There is an updated version of the bill. It is not prepared at this point and the target of the bill to start which would be on a basis to be made available in an omnibus fashion to the entire world would start out with the Independent States and with Africa.

With that, I would like to answer any questions you have and appreciate the time you have given me and would hope that you would find favor in the legislation and help me with it.

Thank you very much, Mr. Chairman.

Chairman FRANK. Thank you.

[The prepared statement of Mr. Traficant can be found in the appendix.]

We will be asking the Export-Import Bank to give us their opinion on this. We will be dealing with it in the spring.

As to the funding, the question will be whether we would authorize it up to a certain amount or whether we would actually sequester a certain amount of funds that could be used only for this.

With regard to the appropriation, of course, we don't do that. The Appropriations Subcommittee does. In fairness to them, they are somewhat squeezed right now especially as it looks like they will be accommodating the NADBank in their appropriation. That will be added to it.

We will be pursuing it further. I appreciate your offer to work with us on it. We will take you up on that in the spring.

Mr. Bereuter.

Mr. BEREUTER. Two quick questions, Mr. Traficant.

Thank you very much for your testimony. I know that you are modifying your amendment now. You mentioned I believe that you have worked out a way to negate the net transfer of U.S. jobs. How do you do that?

Mr. TRAFICANT. The legislation calls for that to be developed and it states that the purpose of the bill is not to do that and there shall be an enforcement mechanism placed in it to be sure the jobs aren't going and the products not coming back.

I envision the program whereby we would more or less help to get these joint ventures started and the products we send there and the products made there are designed for their market and to be consumed in their market. They are not to be exported back to America and not designed nor our small businesses to be sending their jobs there to run these companies.

It would be the technical assistance that would be provided to those small business entities within these two particular countries to start and they would be advised on how to move forward with their particular programs. If you could see the types of ventures started there are not limited to—it deals with manufacturing, with energy, it could deal with a number of things, and it is not limited and it is open for the tailoring of those people who would be enforcing it.

Mr. BEREUTER. I noticed that. Thank you.

I was going to ask you about the limitation to U.S. citizenship, but I see that you have that. Over 50 percent must be owned by U.S. citizens. The joint venture you anticipate would it have to be 50/50 or do you leave flexibility, or do you have thoughts on that?

Mr. TRAFICANT. I think the subcommittee is much better versed than I am on it. I have presented just a recommendation pursuant to an idea that I have. I think it could work, could be a commercial improvement.

We could touch more people with a limited amount of money. We don't have a lot of money. What we are doing with the kinds of appropriations we are coming out with, we are coming out with big bucks and not necessarily hitting as many people as possible.

I think this is educational as well, and it puts in focus an opportunity for people to learn free market production of foods and services, and making them profitable. That is what our purpose is with our Foreign Aid Program. I think that is what this program could do.

On the enforcement end, you can beef it up. We will accept any ideas you have.

Mr. BEREUTER. Thank you very much for your innovation.

Chairman FRANK. Thank you, Mr. Traficant.

Next we will hear from our panel. Ms. Levine, Mr. Ford, Ms. Bradford, Mr. Medina, Mr. Ulrich, please take your seats.

We will begin with Deputy Assistant Secretary Levine.

STATEMENT OF SUSAN B. LEVINE, DEPUTY ASSISTANT SECRETARY FOR INTERNATIONAL DEVELOPMENT, DEBT AND ENVIRONMENT, U.S. DEPARTMENT OF THE TREASURY

Ms. LEVINE. Thank you.

Increasing procurement opportunities for U.S. firms with Multilateral Development Banks is an extremely important issue for the U.S. Treasury.

To date, the United States has already done fairly well in this area particularly in absolute dollar terms, which should be the case since we are the largest contributor. Nevertheless, improving U.S. performance in this area is a key item on this administration's agenda for change in the Multilateral Development Banks.

Other agencies will clearly have major roles to play in this process. The Department of Commerce and the Trade and Development Agency are particularly valuable sources of support and technical expertise.

When talking about procurement we should do so in the international context. Last year the United States exported more than $619 billion in goods and services. Between 1987 and 1991, U.S. exports were the primary engine of growth in our domestic economy accounting for 39 percent of the increase in our Gross Domestic Product over that period.

We benefit when we create freer and more open international trading systems within which the global economy can grow more rapidly.

Each percentage point increase in growth in other G–7 countries will result in more than $10 billion in U.S. exports each year.

We believe that full participation of developing countries in the global trading system will increase U.S. exports by an additional $200 billion over the next 10 years.

This year the Multilateral Development Banks will lend over $45 billion to developing countries. Most of this money has come from funds that are raised in private capital market at no cost to the U.S. Government.

Loan commitments have gone to more than 100 borrowing countries in Asia, Africa, Latin America, and in central and Eastern Europe and the former Soviet Union.

The Multilateral Development Banks make loan commitments in many economic areas and sectors. I will cite some statistics. Agricultural and rural development accounted for $3.3 billion of funds received or 13.8 percent of total lending. Transportation was $3.2 billion or 13.4 percent. Education totaled $2 billion or 8.5 percent. Urban development was also $2 billion, and population health and nutrition was $1.8 billion or 7.6 percent. Clearly, this is a market of such size and diversity that we cannot afford to stay out of it.

Measuring the U.S. performance is an interesting and often complex methodology. The United States has been in absolute dollar terms the most successful performer in procurement of the G–7 countries. The first chart at the end of my statement shows that the United States was estimated to have $2.2 billion of procurement in the most recent fiscal years.

We did a return on investment calculation to try to ascertain how well we did relative to the dollars put in and saw that the United States performed better than Japan or Canada on that basis, but not quite as well as some of the European G–7 countries by virtue of their being more export driven economies, and, in the case of the World Bank, having the closest relationship with the African countries, where a lot of the procurement dollars go.

Behind the figures I have cited, lie a multitude of individual cases in which U.S. firms have won contract awards for MDB financed contracts.

For example, McDermott International of New Orleans is a very large firm with extensive international experience. In 1989, it led an international consortium which won a $407 million contract to carry out the Oso offshore oil condensate project in Nigeria. Of that amount, $265 million has come directly to the United States over the past 3 years to pay for compressors, generators, and other goods and services needed to complete the project.

The award of this contract has had a very positive impact on the economy of New Orleans; 400 people have worked on the contract there and 30 others have worked on site in Nigeria, and still more were engaged in transporting barges and other equipment needed at the site.

The positive impact was felt in other parts of the country due to the activities of subcontractors and suppliers engaged by McDermott. The compressors for the project came from Dresser Industries of New York, the turbine generators came from General Electric of California, and other important equipment came from Crowley Machinery in the State of Washington.

There have been many other large disbursements as you can imagine, and the U.S. firms that have received relatively large disbursements on World Bank projects a number of very different firms including American Cast Iron Pipe from Birmingham, Alabama; U.S. Chemical Resources from Tampa, Florida; Caterpillar from Peoria; and Cargill, Inc. from Minneapolis. Each received contracts of around $10 million to $12 million.

A number of awards have also gone to consulting engineering firms: Morrison-Knudsen of San Francisco; Stokes Engineering of Weston, Connecticut; and Deleuw Cather of Chicago.

U.S. accounting firms have also done well in the MDBs: Deloitte, Haskins and Sells; Peat Marwick; Arthur D. Little; and Price Waterhouse, to name a few.

We do not have separate statistics on minority- and women-owned firms, but last March we do know that the Africa Development Bank's Board of Directors approved a project for $2.3 million which resulted in a contract being awarded to Theragen, Inc., of Capital Heights, Maryland. In recent years, two U.S. minority-owned investment banks, Pryor McClendon and Courts and Doley Securities, have served as comanaging underwriters for African Development Bank Yankee bond offerings.

Let me turn to the financial services sector, the industry from which I originally came. Since 1989, the MDBs have raised more than $62 billion in the capital markets. Of this amount, nearly $50 billion or close to 80 percent was either managed or comanaged by U.S. firms.

The environmental services industry is another key area which stands to derive significant benefits from the MDBs' greatly increased emphasis on environmental work. United States firms have a strong technological lead vis-a-vis other countries in many important areas.

The procurement benefits that I have just outlined are really only the tip of the MDB iceberg. On average, MDB financing has represented about 40 percent of the total cost of individual projects. The rest of the financing has come from other sources such as export promotion agencies and even more has come from the borrowing countries themselves.

This additional financing is shown in the third chart at the end of my statement. It is directly related to MDB lending activity which in many cases gives U.S. suppliers an important opportunity for further business which is not reflected in the MDB reporting systems.

MDB statistics do not always capture procurement benefits accruing to the United States. This is the case when U.S. firms bid through their foreign subsidiaries or as part of a joint venture through or subcontracting arrangement with foreign firms.

For example, Caterpillar has told us that there have been several instances in which World Bank statistics did not fully capture the amount of business that had accrued to their firm.

There will always be some degree of distortion in any complex statistical process. From our point of view, it is more useful to focus on improving our outreach to the U.S. business community and on assuring that U.S. firms are treated fairly in the awarding of MDB contracts.

Our executive directors and alternates are instructed to make business development and exports one of their highest priorities in the MDBs.

Within Treasury, we have created a new position, Assistant Director for Business Development and Exports. This position has been filled by a senior career official. We now have two professional staff members working on these types of issues at Treasury.

We are also working to improve interagency support for MDB business matters. Commerce has already assigned an additional commercial service officer to work with the office of the U.S. Executive Director of the African Development Bank and an additional environmental procurement officer is now in the Office of the U.S. Executive Director of the Asian Development Bank.

Additional commercial service staff is expected at the other banks in the near future. The concept of one-stop shopping at the MDBs has been adopted at the Commerce Department in order to facilitate the assistance provided to U.S. business.

We are also working closely with the Trade and Development Agency to support U.S. consulting engineers and other management consultants at the earliest stages of the project cycle.

Since the beginning of 1993, the MDBs and the U.S. Government have sponsored or participated in more than 150 seminars or conferences designed to encourage participation of U.S. firms.

These conferences and seminars have been very useful in promoting U.S. business. We plan to continue them in the future. We are very interested, however, in developing new mechanisms for involving the private sector more actively in our work with the MDBs and in refining our approach to different sectors of the U.S. business community.

For example, we are making preliminary plans now for a seminar, targeted at small- and medium-size businesses with a special focus on minority- and women-owned firms, that we hope will take place in Chicago in the first quarter of next year.

What we are doing within Treasury is putting much more emphasis on the commercial aspect of our participation in the banks. In some cases, the most useful thing we can do is get out of the way and let the other government agencies and U.S. business firms do the jobs they know how to do much better than we.

The final point I would like to make is that we must also act to meet our financial obligations to the MDBs. At this time, as you know, we have arrears in excess of $818 million. These arrears will certainly interfere with the achievement of all our important policy objectives within the MDBs. This includes our long-term ability to generate greater commercial opportunities. It is important that we begin to reduce our arrears over the next several years.

Thank you.

[The prepared statement of Ms. Levine can be found in the appendix.]

Chairman FRANK. Our next witness is Mr. Charles Ford, who is the Acting Director General of the U.S. and Foreign Commercial Service of the International Trade Administration, Department of Commerce.

STATEMENT OF CHARLES FORD, ACTING DIRECTOR GENERAL, U.S. AND FOREIGN COMMERCIAL SERVICE, INTERNATIONAL TRADE ADMINISTRATION, DEPARTMENT OF COMMERCE

Mr. FORD. Mr. Chairman, let me add three brief comments to hopefully complement the testimony of mine and make the basic points that I have included in the written statement.

First, I think the key point is that we share the subcommittee's concern and perspective on the need to do more for business opportunities in the Multilateral Development Banks. I think in recent years at the Commerce Department, we have recognized this opportunity and have also recognized in recent months as we have worked with Secretary Brown and the Trade Promotion Coordinating Committee that there is much more we can do to focus our efforts and outreach to the business community in this major overseas opportunity.

We are redoubling our efforts to more aggressively address the specific needs of private sector companies competing for Multilateral Development Bank projects. As we now understand those needs, they are for greater access to timely and substantive Multilateral Development Bank project information, and to enhance outreach to all companies in the United States to make sure they are aware of these opportunities.

With regard to small- and minority-owned businesses, we have recently had a very successful seminar where we worked with the Pennsylvania Commerce and Minority Affairs Agency to arrange a seminar in Philadelphia for opportunities at the European Bank as well as the Asian Development Bank. Other needs of the companies particularly involve representation by U.S. officials at the bank and the Embassies on their behalf when they are up against very strong foreign competition.

As we face the need in Commerce to create a new aggressive Multilateral Development Bank operation, we will be consulting actively in the coming weeks with the business community and with our colleagues in the interagency process to better understand what companies expect from us as we look to support them overseas in this area.

Second, I would like to focus on the President's National Export Strategy that was announced by President Clinton and Secretary Brown, the result of a major 19-agency interagency effort in September that focused in specifically on the need for a more aggressive effort by all of our agencies in support of these initiatives. There were three key recommendations that I would highlight. One is the need in Commerce for a single aggressive Multilateral Development Bank operation to deal with business promotion and outreach to the U.S. business community to make sure that we have in place the counseling, information, and advocacy support that our companies need as they go after this business opportunity. We are in the process now of creating this new office within the U.S. and Foreign Commercial Service to concentrate in one spot in the International Trade Administration in Washington and in the overseas networks and in our domestic offices, this capability to better outreach to the U.S. business communities.

Two, increase the liaison support for the Executive Directors at the MDBs. You have heard what we have done in the past; over the course of the coming year we will be doubling our presence at the World Bank and the Inter-American Development Bank and continue to look for additional resources for the three banks overseas.

Three, and this is a particular challenge that we are working closely with the Export-Import Bank, TDA, and OPIC is to integrate Multilateral Development Bank opportunities into our broader U.S. Export Finance Program. We are in the process domestically of creating four pilot "one-stop shops" to improve the delivery of our export services to the business clients and we want to make sure we are including information on Multilateral Development Bank business opportunities.

The final part of our effort here as a result of the President's export strategy is to initiate a more aggressive outreach and information campaign to the U.S. business community in this country and to be there for them when they come to the banks to explore the opportunities that do exist.

There are many success stories that I have included in my written statement. I won't repeat those examples here.

I do think we are very sensitive to two aspects here. As we provide the support to the U.S. business community, it is important for us as we spend the money to have an understanding of what are our results, where have we been successful, where do we need to do more. We are instituting a performance measurement system that will increasingly allow us in the coming year to have a better handle on what has been the result of our efforts in terms of information outreach services we are providing, where our intervention was particularly successful in creating a successful U.S. export opportunity.

I have included some of those in the statement, but I think it is important to have an understanding of not only what are the results but what have we learned from this effort to continue to improve our services to U.S. business.

Chairman FRANK. Thank you, Mr. Ford.

[The prepared statement of Mr. Ford can be found in the appendix.]

Next we will hear from Barbara Bradford, who is the Regional Director of the U.S. Trade and Development Agency.

STATEMENT OF BARBARA R. BRADFORD, REGIONAL DIRECTOR, TRADE AND DEVELOPMENT AGENCY

Ms. BRADFORD. Mr. Chairman, I would like to take a little different tack and tell you a little bit about a very specific program that we have started at the Trade and Development Agency to try and increase the share of U.S. procurement from the Multilateral Development Banks. I would like to introduce you to TDA, which doesn't normally testify before this subcommittee.

TDA is a commercially oriented foreign assistance agency. That means we don't just give money away, we spend money in order to bring money back to the United States.

We work directly with Commerce and State in their efforts to increase U.S. exports from the United States and to achieve our foreign policy goals. We are a strong supporter of the President's efforts to increase U.S. exports and are an active participant in the TPCC.

TDA is appearing before the subcommittee today in its role as a U.S. agency which is actively involved in helping U.S. firms to increase their share of procurement from the MDBs.

These activities, however, represent a relatively minor part of TDA's overall program. Its main program positions U.S. firms in large capital projects in developing countries so that U.S. goods and services will be used in the implementation of those projects. We work with projects financed mainly by MDBs as well as projects which will be financed by the host country itself or by the private sector.

We have placed funds at several of the MDBs. We have five funds at four different banks in order to gain information about bank projects, and to have U.S. participation in developing the parameters for bank projects. Since 1986, TDA has put a total of $11.6 million into these five funds.

TDA retains veto power over how its funds are spent, but it responds to bank requests for U.S. consultants to help in the preparation of bank projects. U.S. presence in the preparation of the project makes it more likely that U.S. equipment will be used in that project, or at least will not be precluded from use in the project by narrow equipment specifications, than if there were no U.S. consultants present.

The consultants which we fund are interviewed by TDA once their work for the bank is concluded. The consultants are asked about the potential for U.S. exports to the bank project and to the relevant foreign country in general. We provide this information to the U.S. business community through our newsletter, the "TDA Bi-Weekly." TDA backs up this information with training for U.S. firms on how to compete and win bank procurement awards.

The preliminary figures given us by the banks show that the funds provide between $40 to $178 in U.S. exports for every dollar that we put into the trust funds. However, establishment and replenishment do not automatically achieve a higher proportion of procurement. The banks are very complex organizations and effective use of the funds depends more on how they are administered than the amount of money in them.

TDA has developed close working relationships with the banks. The result is a significant leveraging mechanism involving a relatively small sum of money that has a significant effect on U.S. exports. United States exports means a strong U.S. economy which translates into steady U.S. jobs.

TDA is able to provide early information about bank projects to U.S. firms. But, TDA's work must be followed up by a thorough and sophisticated approach by U.S. firms when it comes time to compete for and win bank procurement. It is well worth it since the banks represent a market of well over $20 billion a year. TDA is dedicated to increasing the U.S. share of MDB procurement.

Thank you.

[The prepared statement of Ms. Bradford can be found in the appendix.]

Chairman FRANK. Thank you.

I neglected to say that if there is no objection, all of the written statements and the supporting material will be put in the record. There does not appear to be any objection.

The next witness is Mr. Manuel A. Medina. I know he is actively involved in shipping and economic activity between the United States and Africa, specifically Cape Verde, and he speaks to us as a businessman who has had significant experience pioneering in international activity and is interested in sharing with us his views about what we can do at the Federal level to enhance that kind of activity.

Mr. Medina.

STATEMENT OF MANUEL A. MEDINA, PRESIDENT, CAPE VERDEAN-AMERICAN IMPORT/EXPORT, INC.

Mr. MEDINA. Thank you Mr. Chairman.

I would like to compliment Ms. Levine, Mr. Charles Ford, and Ms. Barbara Bradford because it is what we need in terms of small business to go forward. I have only a few points I want to make and I will submit the rest of my testimony for the record.

My family-owned shipping company operates the only scheduled ocean freight service between the United States of America and the Cape Verde Islands, West Africa. Since mid-1988 the company has moved over 888,000 cubic feet of cargo to West Africa and generated in excess of $2.1 million in documented business in the Greater New Bedford area. At the present time we employ 30 people.

As a small minority firm we are encouraged by all of the talk out of Washington about the role of export promotion in the economic recovery plans of the Clinton administration. Shipping companies like mine will be secondary beneficiaries, after manufacturing and distribution companies, of any sustained expansion in the export sector. My city of New Bedford is an economically depressed area which in spite of its excellent port and existing export capabilities has been living on a hands-to-mouth basis for years.

In so many places like New Bedford there seems to be a major gap between what our government is talking about and what the government is actually doing to support the manufacturing sector while simultaneously aggressively backing up the efforts of private business people to open up and expand foreign markets. If the United States is serious about expanding exports, why do small companies like mine have to wrestle through so much red tape in order to get information about financing exports?

What do we have to do to get our Embassies behind our efforts to introduce U.S. products and get trading relationships off the grounds no matter how small they may appear to be?

I believe it has to do with the lack of creativity to use the resources America has and the lack of determination to "back up" the individuals and private companies who put themselves on the line trying to make it in the export business.

New Bedford has centuries-old cultural attachments to many parts of the world which are now poised for economic growth. The city is filled with abandoned but usable manufacturing space and a labor force still driven by a traditional work ethic.

Like many other cities in our country, there are small businessmen who have long cultural ties to other parts of the world. Our government should be aggressively encouraging entrepreneurs and small companies with overseas cultural ties to do business abroad. But the reality is that for small U.S. companies trying to make it as exporters, more often than not we are out there on our own. Whenever my company has discovered a potentially profitable new venture we invariably lose valuable time in our efforts to secure financing. So often by the time we find the financing another larger firm has taken advantage of our research and investment of time. Many of the opportunities for breaking into export sales of which we are aware have been lost to us because of the way EEC and other trading blocs "take care of their own."

In our case, many of the projects we want to supply receive their funding through EEC countries' foreign assistance programs and have the requirement that only EEC goods be produced. Is there something that the French and the rest of the EEC know about opening up foreign markets and supporting their small companies that our government might learn?

In the last analysis, to really expand the number of companies involved in the export sector our government needs to institute "hand-to-hand outreach" programs which put good managers together with small groups of people who are then systematically helped to take advantage of business situations and programs as they occur. Federal programs need to be designed from the "bottom up" if they are ever to achieve any sustainable impact and growth in the New Bedfords of America.

Thank you, Mr. Chairman.

Chairman FRANK. Thank you, Mr. Medina.

74-137 O - 94 - 2

[The prepared statement of Mr. Medina can be found in the appendix.]

Mr. Robert Ulrich, vice president of Parsons Brinckerhoff International, is testifying on behalf of the American Consulting Engineers Council.

STATEMENT OF ROBERT ULRICH, VICE PRESIDENT AND GROUP MARKETING MANAGER, PARSONS BRINCKERHOFF INTERNATIONAL, ON BEHALF OF THE AMERICAN CONSULTING ENGINEERS COUNCIL

Mr. ULRICH. Thank you.

Two years ago, the American Consulting Engineers Council was invited by Congress to identify those areas of MDB procurement that could use improvement. Soon afterwards, Congressmen Bereuter and Gejdenson attached amendments to last year's OPIC Reauthorization bill that addressed the problems raised in our testimony.

The amendments established technical assistance funds at the MDBs; expanded the procurement staff of the U.S. Executive Directors' Offices, and called for greater accessibility to procurement information and internal bank documents.

Today, we understand that a reference room will soon open that provides project information to industry.

We understand that the increase in procurement staff has not yet occurred but we continue to believe that we will see new people in those offices in the very near future.

Turning to trust funds, the Trade and Development Agency has established technical assistance funds at all MDBs, but these funds need to be capitalized at a higher level. It is simply an issue of improving the return on our existing investment. Because of our testimony and the serious manner in which it was received, the Treasury Department through the efforts of Nelson Coar, has created a better rapport with the private sector and appears genuinely interested in trade issues that concern the industry.

I would like to just make three fundamental points which serve to highlight the importance and effectiveness of the Multilateral Development Banks to industry as well as to the overall U.S. economic interests.

First, I would like to explain how the U.S. engineering industry drives trade by specifying other U.S. services and goods. Second, I would like to talk about the importance of increasing the level of U.S. trusts funds; and finally I would like to touch on what we believe should be the necessary support elements of the U.S. and Foreign Commercial Service personnel who are employed by U.S. offices at banks.

The main purpose of the MDBs is to create and sustain economic stability in developing countries as part of that overarching process, the MDBs finance infrastructure projects which help support that stability. Subsequently, those projects create markets for U.S. firms in those developing countries. The potential to export is great and affects a variety of areas—power, telecommunications, environment, education, and transportation, to name a few.

We know it is difficult during these budget constrained times to talk about foreign assistance programs, but I want to make very clear that what I am talking about is not foreign assistance. What I am talking about is a comprehensive strategy on how to level the playing field for U.S. firms pursuing overseas work in the Multilateral Development Bank marketplace. I am speaking about export promotion.

The engineering community plays a significant role in increasing the volume of U.S. exports around the world. Engineering services are the "opening wedge" of the entire export process. The fact is that when you commit to the engineering of a project, you are making the first hard money commitment in the project process. And that commitment incorporates the development of standards and specifications which will dictate the ability of U.S. suppliers and manufacturers to compete for "follow-on" contracts. When U.S. engineers develop project standards and specifications, they are developed to international levels and that is the norm in the domestic market here in the United States.

When the Japanese or the Europeans develop those specs they are to European or Japanese specifications. Helping the U.S. engineer get to the table is, in effect, helping U.S. industry as a whole.

Our international competition is well aware of this opening wedge and the relationship between engineering and how they relate to exports. The Japanese, the Germans, and the French among others, are aggressively competing with our firms and have caused the United States share of the international construction market to decline over the past several years. I think it is important to note that the U.S. engineering and architectural and construction industries together account for some 15 percent of the U.S. gross national product. We are not running away from our competitors or being outdone technically; we are having problems finding ways to compete financially.

The United States, in our opinion, could vastly increase its market share if U.S. funds finance small but early portions of capital projects. In order for U.S. firms to capture a greater portion of the MDB market, it must increase the level of these trust funds, supplemental to that of the Trade and Development Agency, and they must be devoted specifically to engineering and architectural services. Trust funds give the U.S. firms the first shot at a major project.

We can compete more effectively with our foreign competition because trusts finance the initial portion of the project, which gives U.S. firms higher visibility with the foreign government, the host government, when the project moves into the implementation phase. Simply put, trust funds enhance a U.S. firm's chances at winning a project.

It is nothing more than an insurance policy. If I look at the EBRD, the United States owns a 10 percent share of the bank. We are the single largest country shareholder at that bank but when it comes to procurement of engineering services, I believe we provided a total in trust funds of $1.1 million last year for U.S. firms. Conversely, not only do the member nations of the European Community collectively provide roughly $40 million for that same purpose, but certain countries also have established individual trusts in that bank reserved specifically for their engineering firms to bid on projects. Competitor nations have recognized the importance of the trust funds to assure getting their shot at a project.

In the case of my own firm, Parsons Brinckerhoff, we are the number one ranked U.S. transport engineering consultant. We have been shortlisted for technical assignments on three different occasions by the European Bank for Reconstruction and Development. On each occasion, we found out that a French or a German firm had won the job by going back to their trust funds.

Trust funds help to promote and support the national interest, whosoever's national interest it might be. We need more trust funds and we need more U.S. funding to obtain a larger share of the MDB marketplace.

In 1993, the World Bank cofinanced 118 projects at a cost of $11 billion. Member firms or nations cofinanced an additional $7.7 billion that drove $35 billion in projects. When you hear that number, you realize how important it is for the United States to participate in these procurements on an equal footing with our competitors.

I think it is important to note that as a U.S. firm, when I get put in this position I quite literally have no place in Washington to turn to. As much as the Export-Import Bank or TDA have been exceptionally helpful to us, the fact is that our competition is simply doing more in the way of financing projects.

If I could turn to the U.S. Executive Director's offices, we know they are there to look after the interest of the United States and it is through these offices that a lot of export promotion for U.S. products and services take place. In order to perform these tasks effectively, a U.S. Executive Director should be stationed during their tenure at the bank on location, not here in Washington.

The U.S. Foreign and Commercial Service and its staff support the MDB's U.S. Executive Directors and these positions are critical to the U.S. private sector because they represent a vital link between business and government; but it is time that we look at this part of the process as the rest of the world does—as a business. And that is exactly what it is when you are in procurement.

The key to the successful pursuit of a World Bank or Multilateral Development Bank project is accurate and timely information as well as the ability of the U.S. foreign and commercial service to be proactive rather than reactive. Increased staffing levels for procurement specialists in the U.S. Executive Directors office will improve the quality and quantity of information that we need to pursue these opportunities.

I want to emphasize that U.S. engineering firms are engaged in the international market and are holding their own based on quality, expertise, and a commitment to the profession. We are not losing projects based on our technology or our program management skills.

In fact, I can tell you that U.S. technical skills are highly sought after throughout the world. But when our competitors bring the full support of their government through tied aid trust funds into the picture, the rules of the game drastically change.

Foreign governments bring with them a sound understanding that their engineering industry is a vehicle for export promotion of their country's products and services. Unlike our competition, my colleagues and I find that we have few places in our government to turn to thwart the challenges posed to us overseas. While the U.S. Government's support for the engineering industry has improved dramatically over the last 10 years, we still need a commitment that matches our own in terms of not just staying competitive, but winning.

Finally, I ask your support to: One, increase United States TDA funding levels and subsequently, the trust funds levels of MDBs; two, that Eximbank programs be bettered to meet the engineering industry's needs; and finally that appropriate staff levels be kept at the USED's offices of the MDBs.

Thank you very much.

[The prepared statement of Mr. Ulrich can be found in the appendix.]

Chairman FRANK. Thank you.

We will break now because we have a vote. We will come back and ask you our questions then.

Ms. WATERS. I ask unanimous consent to enter my statement.

Chairman FRANK. Without objection.

Ms. Waters has been one of those who has been most interested in the subject, and unfortunately there are a number of things going on right now that are competing; for example, the Abortion Clinic Access bill. The Chair must say that my experiment with afternoon hearings was not one of the better ideas.

We will go back to the morning next year and have less competition of this sort. We will include Ms. Waters' statement in the record and we will be in recess.

[Brief recess.]

[The prepared statement of Ms. Waters can be found in the appendix.]

Chairman FRANK. I know I should have two members but because when we scheduled this hearing, we did not realize this would be the week before adjournment so that puts stress and strains on it. In fairness to the witnesses who have been very cooperative—I appreciate particularly the administration witnesses agreeing to this format—I am going to ask my questions.

Let me begin by asking the three administration witnesses to comment on what Mr. Ulrich said. I realize some of this has to do with Exim and we will be talking to them as well. That is the next question.

First, his point was that with regard to trust funds, we are probably small compared to others. Mr. Medina said he also ran into some problems where the EC was more protective. I realize that this goes beyond just the question of the multilaterals, although the trust fund does affect that.

Let me ask the three administration witnesses, are we underdoing the trust funds issue vis-a-vis the other nations?

Ms. Levine.

Ms. LEVINE. What we have typically tried to do is advocate that all trust funds be untied because where the trust funds are untied, the U.S. does very well in competing for those funds.

For example, at the EBRD, there are two untied trust funds: Japan and Taiwan and we have done quite well in getting business from these two funds. Were we in fact thinking of putting more tied trust funds in place, we would advocate that they be administered by TDA.

To the extent that trust funds are tied, we would look to TDA. It is also a budget issue. There are limited resources.

How do you allocate them? We would like all trust funds to be untied in order to level the playing field and then the United States does well according to our experience.

Chairman FRANK. What about those countries who refuse to untie them? Are we able to defend our people? I realize the goal for them to be untied is the best, and really untied rather than with Exim where there are the pseudo untied, the ones said to be untied but were de facto tied.

I realize you are talking about things that are not tied in. What about with regard to those countries that refuse to untie their trust funds? What do we do to help our people in those situations?

Ms. LEVINE. We refer them to TDA.

Chairman FRANK. Ms. Bradford, let's go to you. Have we—because this is not your autonomous decision—have we in the budget process given you sufficient trust funds to be able to protect Americans against losing business they would otherwise get because of this?

Ms. BRADFORD. Our funds for the trust fund come out of our general budget. We find that our regular program is very effective and much faster disbursing than our trust fund money is.

However, that doesn't mean we don't want to put money into the trust funds. The trouble is that the United States doesn't really have a mechanism to go after all the commercial opportunities that the bank provides both through cofinancing and through technical assistance.

AID represents the American Government for the bank and they, due to their mandate, go after humanitarian opportunities.

Chairman FRANK. AID represents the American Government to which bank, the World Bank?

Ms. BRADFORD. In terms of cofinancing and technical assistance. Due to their mandate, they go after the humanitarian opportunities.

Chairman FRANK. So you are telling me that we have a gap here and this is probably something I ought to talk about with Mr. Gejdenson and his subcommittee. I think we agree that the ideal is no tying, no distorting of the market by financial subsidies, but that where there are some we are going to the fight without weapons. Mr. Ford.

Mr. FORD. I was going to say that the issue of how to cover that gap is something that was debated long and hard in the administration as we put together the national export strategy in the trade promotion coordinating committee. There was a discussion of the need to have some tied aid on capital projects.

Chairman FRANK. We are using multilateral development banks as a jumping off point because we have jurisdiction but that is an artificial way to talk about it.

We ought to talk about all forms——

Mr. FORD. It was a decision to do it on a modest basis in the war chest of Exim and money for TDA to deal with feasibility studies, a decision to consolidate and enhance that.

Chairman FRANK. You say we have the war chest at Exim. What about trust funds?

Ms. BRADFORD. Trust funds at TDA definitely are tied to U.S. consultants.

Chairman FRANK. How much could you commit in trust funds? What is the maximum available to you? Can it be whatever you want? Is there a limit? You have an overall budget, is there a limit within that budget as to how much can be for trust funds?

Ms. BRADFORD. No. The trouble is that our mainstream program is much more effective and quicker dispersing than are the funds at the various Multilateral Development Banks. Although we think it is important to go after procurement at the Multilateral Development Banks, certainly our mainstream program——

Chairman FRANK. What kind of scoring do you get for the trust funds? For every $10 million of trust funds, how much would you get charged by CBO? Is it 100 percent?

Ms. BRADFORD. It is 100 percent.

Chairman FRANK. So there is no recovery because that has to go to offset the subsidy. It does seem to me we might want to, in scoring that, deduct at least the government's share of what the gain would be for the company. There is a certain tax revenue.

Ms. BRADFORD. We believe there is a tremendous tax revenue just with the export numbers alone.

Chairman FRANK. So it is a matter of accounting. That is something we ought to be looking at. I gather we have a cap.

Mr. Ford, you said we have the war chest, but in general the decision was that we couldn't afford to do very much in this area?

Mr. FORD. In general, the decision was to have a modest attempt to deal with those practices we couldn't get at but to continue to try to force——

Chairman FRANK. I must say the only way—the best way I can think of to force them to stop it is to tie them, literally tie the funds and to equal them because exhortation seems to be an unlikely tool here. So I think we have an issue that until and unless we are prepared to do the same thing they are doing we will be disadvantaged and the best way to get rid of these things—I think this is the arms race analogy—the best way to make sure these things aren't used is to have some kind of equality so that it is in nobody's interest to do it and we all save the money. That is not where we are?

Mr. FORD. We are not completely there.

Chairman FRANK. Feasibility studies——

Ms. BRADFORD. That is what we do. TDA positions U.S. firms in large projects overseas and the way we do it is we go to the sponsors of those projects and say, look if you will use U.S. engineering firms to do the work for the planning and feasibility studies we will pick up the tab. That puts U.S. engineering firms in on the ground floor of the projects.

Hopefully, they will write the specifications to U.S. equipment. We find that more of the goods and services that go into that project are going to be United States than if say the French or someone else has done the feasibility study. So all over the developing world we are trying to get those opportunities for U.S. firms.

Chairman FRANK. Mr. Ulrich, does that work in your experience?

Mr. ULRICH. Absolutely. TDA has been the difference between our winning and losing on any number of occasions.

Chairman FRANK. I ask you this question, because we have budgetary constraints. Ms. Bradford is saying they had to choose between the feasibility study model and trust funds. Do you think they are making the right choice?

I know you would rather have them have more money to do both. In the constraints that are around, what do you think?

Mr. ULRICH. Given the limited money they have, they are exceptionally effective the way they are.

Ms. LEVINE. I just wanted to add one thing. We have been successful in achieving some untied trust funds. For example, the United States this past year got $108 million of funding from the World Bank. It was the largest amount for consultancy and other types of projects from their trust funds.

Chairman FRANK. How did we do that? These are the World Bank's or countries'?

Ms. LEVINE. World Bank untied trust funds and we got the largest share. We got $108 million, which is substantial.

Chairman FRANK. Mr. Medina, you talked about your frustration dealing with the European Community. Is it your experience that the European Community protects its own companies more firmly than the United States does?

Mr. MEDINA. Yes, I believe so, sir. Because about 6 months ago my company tried to bid for a powerplant in Cape Verde, and they gave us 6 weeks to answer to their proposal with American goods.

Chairman FRANK. Where was this?

Mr. MEDINA. In Cape Verde. And we came to find out that the European Community market financing for that project, they had been preapproved and also they said only goods procured in the European market could be. It specifically said that, no Asian, no Americans.

Chairman FRANK. Did you approach AID perhaps to see if we could match that?

Mr. MEDINA. No. At that time, we didn't because we didn't have enough time.

Chairman FRANK. We don't have AID here but we have three other agencies. Is there a place that an American company should go in a situation like that, where they believe they are in danger of losing a contract that they could win on the merits because of some element of subsidy in a competitor's home country operation?

Mr. FORD. I would say generally what we advise is that in our Commerce district offices, we are trying to put finance into our marketing counseling as a place to raise the issue and are working more closely with the Export-Import Bank to see if there is an answer.

Chairman FRANK. And it would be the Export-Import Bank that would have to have the capacity to do that, isn't that what the war chest is for?

Ms. LEVINE. And if it is an MDB project, that is clearly what the executive director's office is there for. One of the things that we have——

Chairman FRANK. OK. If you go to the executive director, what can he or she legally do?

Ms. LEVINE. If it is an MDB project we want to make sure bidding processes are fair, they are supposed to be open and competitive. One side benefit of the World Bank's recent change in information policy is that information on projects will be out earlier. It is important that U.S. firms know about a project early.

Chairman FRANK. Mr. Medina, was this one of the things with the Cape Verde project?

Mr. MEDINA. It had been financed in the EEC.

Chairman FRANK. That is a problem where they are financing themselves. Would our executive directors when they approach a situation like that—are they empowered legally to say to the multidevelopment bank, you can't do this?

Ms. LEVINE. There are practices in place that must be followed for the awarding of contracts, and so it is up to us to make sure that those practices are followed.

Chairman FRANK. When it comes to multilateral development banks, they don't accept money on a tied basis, do they?

Ms. LEVINE. What we were speaking about earlier were trust funds tied where the consulting projects are awarded. The point was well made that if you get involved in a project early, the likely effect is that the larger big awards will go to those who help design the spec. So clearly, early involvement will succeed in getting more of the bigger procurement.

Chairman FRANK. Who would put up the untied funds?

Ms. LEVINE. Japanese, Taiwanese, other countries, us sometimes, if we have resources.

Chairman FRANK. This was a case where other countries put up the funds and we are taking the position that they should not be tied?

Ms. LEVINE. That is correct. For example, in our current negotiations for replenishment of the IDB, we are arguing that trust funds should continue to be untied. We continue to take that stance.

Chairman FRANK. That is not up to the bank. Isn't that up to the donor country? If I were a bank, I would always rather people gave me money without conditions than not. Then the NAFTA debate came up and it turned out that wasn't true on both sides. We are not targeting the banks. It is Japan and the Europeans.

Ms. LEVINE. The Japan Trust Fund is not tied and we have done well there. We continue to argue that they should be untied.

Chairman FRANK. Mr. Bereuter.

Mr. BEREUTER. Thank you, to all of you for your testimony.

Ms. Levine, what is the position of the administration on the creation of trust funds at the MDBs?

Ms. LEVINE. The position again is that we would—if trust funds were to be created, from our point of view, we would like them to be created at TDA. We are not actively advocating creation of additional trust funds. We are just looking at what resources are available right now in this budgetary environment.

Mr. BEREUTER. You say if they are created they should be at TDA. Did I understand that correctly?

Ms. LEVINE. That is correct.

Mr. BEREUTER. What is your position?

Ms. LEVINE. On whether they should be?

Mr. BEREUTER. Yes.

Ms. LEVINE. If there is sufficient money to provide both the funding for the MDBs and additional trust funds, certainly, as our colleagues have said, having that kind of money to provide for consultants is important. We think there are already in place appropriate mechanisms both with the untied trust funds and with TDA.

Mr. BEREUTER. This whole question of the tied aid goes back a long way and the U.S. position has always been that this is not a good thing to proceed with and therefore we are not going to engage in it. If I may say so, it has been a long, almost fruitless process. I guess some people would say it is naive. I would at least say it is naive when you are competing against countries like the French or like the British who do use tied aid routinely. We can stick to our principle position, but it is our export, our business, sector that is the loser.

Let me ask you how much real progress has been made with respect to filling positions? Somewhere in the testimony I got the impression that the new positions authorized for the African and Asian Banks are in place, but does that mean none of the others are?

Mr. FORD. In the African Bank, we now have two officers working. We have increased this in the last year. In the case of the Asian Bank in Manila, we have, with the cooperation of AID, put in a person specifically focused on environmental projects that the Asian Bank is financing in that part of the world. We are recruiting another staff member to join us in the EBRD in London and have committed to have additional staff people in the World Bank and IDB by this summer.

Mr. BEREUTER. By this summer?

Mr. FORD. In the African Bank we have the two officers now.

Mr. BEREUTER. Do you think that is being responsive to have them in place by next summer?

Mr. FORD. We are trying as soon as we can to get officers in rotation to get there. If we can do it sooner we are making the effort to do that.

Mr. BEREUTER. I hope you will have them in place before January 1994. Time is wasting and time is money.

Am I correct in understanding that the person you have at the Asian Development Bank is an AID person that is on contract?

Mr. FORD. The second person we have added, yes.

Mr. BEREUTER. What will happen after that American completes the contract?

Mr. FORD. We will evaluate the program at that time and put in the pipeline immediately to have another person to replace that individual.

Mr. BEREUTER. Mr. Ulrich, what do you think about the idea of eliminating the trust funds? What does your association of consulting engineers think about that?

Mr. ULRICH. In a perfect world, it makes a lot of sense. The fact of the matter is that all of our competitors are using trust funds. The majority are using tied aid trust funds. That fact is that is the reality of the situation. When we run up against that we have to have a way to compete.

Mr. BEREUTER. What do you think that has meant to us, if you have any knowledge of the EBRD and its initial year of operation?

Mr. ULRICH. It has done a number on it. I know for the engineering industry, in the past year we were awarded 2.5 million dollars worth of contracts and I guess TDA had, I believe, $1.1 million in trust funds. So overall we held our own, but I think there is an awful lot more out there. The purchasing power last year was more in the area of about $200 million.

Mr. BEREUTER. The charts which compare the percentage of procurement that we are receiving for U.S. firms are interesting, and I believe there probably has been improvement made, but it seems to me there is a long ways to go. We should be capturing far more than our percentage when it comes to professional services, because we have such a dominant leadership position in professional services in the world.

But we are so competitive, extraordinarily competitive, in almost every area, we ought to be capturing a disproportionate share of those engineering, architectural, planning, all variety of consulting activities. So I hope we are going to set ourselves a very high standard and nothing approximating the percentage of funds that we contribute in that area.

Maybe that might be acceptable when it actually comes to the delivery of hardware and construction, but I would be disappointed even if we set that as an acceptable measuring point.

Ms. Bradford, what can you tell me about the coordination of your programs with the executive directors and their staffs at the various MDBs? What would you like to see happen to improve coordination, or more importantly, effectiveness of our dollars?

Ms. BRADFORD. Sir, actually I think that the coordination at this time is excellent. The executive directors' offices are there to enforce the policy of the United States, which is to have fair and open procurement at the banks.

Frankly, TDA trust funds are there to be tied to U.S. procurement to try to go after as much procurement as we can at those banks and make sure that it is going to the United States. So in a way we tried to work directly with the bank staff level and not with the executive director's office that is interested in fairness and policy. We are in there fighting and trying to get as many U.S. firms winning the procurements as possible.

Mr. BEREUTER. I think that is an important and good distinction.

Are you focused to any special extent on the earliest end of the process at the initial design stage?

Ms. BRADFORD. Yes. The trust funds are the earliest stage at the identification and preparation of the bank projects which will eventually become the loans. In fact, sometimes we do sector work which is even before the actual individual loans are identified. So we are at the very early stage.

Mr. BEREUTER. Let me say I think that is very important and the right place to apply your resources. I have seen situations where we have a European firm in, and they get the earliest stage and everything thereafter is designed for the machine tools and the architectural standards of that particular country's major contractor. So once they get in at the initial stage, the dollars continue to follow.

Ms. BRADFORD. We find that, too. That is the TDA idea, that if you put the engineering firm in early on the project, you will put a U.S. spin on the project.

Mr. BEREUTER. Mr. Ulrich, how will your association monitor the progress of the U.S. Government? Ordinarily the U.S. Government monitors the private sector. I wonder if you could sort of monitor the governmental sector?

Mr. ULRICH. If we were to do that, it would have to be to see what kind of programs we see out of Eximbank that really respond to engineering needs. I think one barometer would be the level of funding at the Trade and Development Agency.

Mr. BEREUTER. I wonder if the council could set up perhaps in conjunction with the American Institute of Architects, and any front-end design kind of association, some kind of panels to monitor the success of the U.S. Government in assisting American business to receive procurement, all kinds of procurement from early design stage through construction, through equipment, through maintenance?

I wonder if that could be something that you would do for your own benefit, and provide us unofficially kind of a yearly progress statement? It could be from a panel or council so that you are not exposing a particular firm to the possible retribution of a too-critical report.

Mr. ULRICH. I appreciate that and we welcome that opportunity. We will take you up on that.

Mr. BEREUTER. Thank you very much. It is not that I don't trust executive branch agencies; I just want to see progress faster than your bosses perhaps are going to let you move and I want to see people in place doing their job and cutting through personnel rigamarole and delay, if at all possible.

Thank you, Mr. Chairman.

Chairman FRANK. Let me follow up on what Mr. Bereuter said.

From your own experience, it strikes me on the question of untied aid versus tied aid and war chests and subsidy, that the ideal would be a world in which none of that existed, but I think you would find Members of Congress overwhelmingly convinced that the only way to get there is in fact to engage in those same kinds of practices because as long as people can get a unilateral advantage in them, they are going to do them.

The analogy for us would be negative campaigning. When I started in politics the prevailing common wisdom was that if people said nasty things about you you should ignore them and rise above them and they would go away. There are a lot of private citizens now who followed that advice. What happens was that people understood that the best way to deal with negative campaigning was to respond and that has done more to restrain people than anything else.

In particular, you have people like Mr. Medina, the people that Mr. Ulrich represents who are outward looking—too many Americans haven't been. It is important to know if someone like Mr. Medina were to come to any Member of Congress, we might want to—I might suggest to the three agencies you might want to make sure that every House Member and every Senator had in his or her office the answer to the question Mr. Medina might ask, which is that I am facing an unfair situation, I can win this contract on my merits but I am not going to get to the merits because of a subsidy.

Most of our Members might not be familiar with the resources and may not be sure where to turn. I think you might want information to circulate so among the things people would have in their district offices would be an answer to that question and people might be ready to do some outreach.

Several of the African-American Members in particular, are interested in meeting with business people in their districts who would be interested in business in Africa or elsewhere. I think you might want to prepare a packet, and if people knew you were available, you might find yourselves getting requests to go to regional meetings where small business people could be told about this.

The other thing is it is obvious from the administration's standpoint we have had a couple of tough fights this year. When the money for the World Bank was included in the appropriation, there was an effort to knock it out. Mr. Bereuter and I participated in an effort on the floor to keep it in and won by 6 votes.

The more you can work with us so that we can show Americans that we are directly benefiting not just as donors but as participants, the likelier we are to be able to sustain that. So when we talk about trying to get a good American share, it is not simply that we are trying to put money in the pockets of people here, although that is a perfectly worthy thing to do, but showing Americans that we are treated fairly in the disbursements of these funds that go overseas is increasingly a synonym for our government being able to continue to supply them.

I agree with Mr. Bereuter when he says that we want to move and have the positions filled, but people at Treasury and State should understand their ability to meet some of their international policy goals will be greatly enhanced by moving in this kind of area so that American business people can become enthusiastic advocates for it.

Mr. BEREUTER. Mr. Chairman, I want to associate myself with your remarks. They are very much on target. There will come a day when we fail to get the appropriations for the MDBs, and, if we fail, in part it will be because we have not extended the message to the members about the advantages that their constituents receive.

You perhaps could take a page from the NASA book. The NASA book can tell us in each major project what contractors in each Congressman's district are benefiting from a contract. McDonnell-Douglas can tell you, the Defense Department can tell you, and it would be very good if the Executive Director of the World Bank, the Asian Development Bank, and so forth could break it down in that kind of politically sensitive, effective way as well.

Chairman FRANK. I will get it to them Monday when my amendment to cut the space station comes up. Many of us have had the experience of having conferences with business people. If you could on an interagency kind of basis: One, give people a place to call if someone walks in; and two, provide information about MDB projects and the contractors in each Member's district benefiting from the contracts, we would be glad to work with you.

Mr. Bereuter, I would be glad to circulate a "Dear Colleague" and say we would like to let you know of resources that are available to you because it is good for the American economy. If some of you would like to get back to us after the first of the year, we would like to pursue that.

Ms. LEVINE. To Mr. Bereuter's comments, that is a very good recommendation and we will start to prepare that information by States so at the very least people will know which State is involved. And the next challenge is, can we go by congressional district and the issue is can we get that information? We will certainly look to see whether that is possible.

Mr. BEREUTER. Thank you. I appreciate that.

Given some of our congressional districts right now, it would not be humanly impossible to define what I have in mind in North Carolina.

Chairman FRANK. He is not here right now.

The hearing is adjourned.

I thank all the panelists. If any of you have anything occur to you in the next week or two that you would like to add by way of a written document or any comments you would like to submit, the record always stays open for a while. And if there is no objection, there will be time to incorporate that.

Sometimes you go home and say I should have told them that, and we would be glad to take it for the permanent record of the hearing.

[Whereupon, at 3:45 p.m., the hearing was adjourned.]

APPENDIX

November 18, 1993

Opening Statement by the Honorable Doug Bereuter at the hearing of the Subcommittee on International Development, Finance, Trade, and Monetary Policy on Procurement by U.S. Firms in Connection with Projects Financed by the Multilateral Development Banks, November 18, 1993.

Mr. Chairman, I am delighted that we are addressing today the subject of procurement in the Multilateral Development Banks (MDBs). This have been an interest of mine for several years, and one on which action was taken on several fronts in the last Congress as a result of a hearing early in 1992 in this Subcommittee. I must especially commend the American Consulting Engineers' Council who testified at that hearing and subsequently drafted a number of recommendations for effective reforms. They worked with Congress and later with the TPCC to develop a more effective approach to procurement in the MDBs.

To summarize some of the legislative actions that have already happened on this subject --

* On October 6, 1992, the Congress passed the Jobs Through Exports Act (H.R. 4996), which included several provisions to help improve the prospects for international exports.

* One provision creates an additional full-time position for a procurement officer from the U.S. Department of Commerce within the office of the U.S. Executive Director at the World Bank and at similar offices in each of the four regional multilateral development banks for Latin America, Africa, Asia, and Eastern Europe. These officers will help

U.S. firms to chase procurement opportunities in the $20 billion-per-year market of projects financed by these institutions in less-developed parts of the world.

* A second provision encourages more U.S. Government funds to be set aside to provide technical assistance "trust funds" so that the multilateral development banks can hire more U.S. professionals as additional consultants to participate in project design and appraisal teams. Since design influences ultimate procurement, many countries have set up such trust funds to give their exporters an edge. The U.S. has had a very small program in the Trade and Development Agency, funded at less than $2 million annually, which has been quite successful in increasing U.S. exports of goods and services. The law encouraged significant expansion of this program.

The testimony today should let the Congress have a status report on implementation of these provisions. In addition I have been pleased to see that the TPCC Report released in late September has identified better facilitation of U.S. procurement at the MDBs as a priority. Let's continue to work together to tap this multi-billion dollar procurement MDB market for U.S. companies.

OPENING STATEMENT OF MAXINE WATERS

Hearing on Multilateral Development Bank Procurement Programs

Mr. Chairman, it seems appropriate that we have this hearing today. After last night's passage of NAFTA, it seems this country's long term economic strategy has crystallized. This Administration believes the path to future prosperity will be derived, even primarily dependent on, the growth and establishment of new export industries.

Some of us, though favoring strong exports, fear that neglect of this countries current manufacturing and industrial base, and a reliance on exports, carries great economic risks. Nonetheless, there is no remaining question that we have shifted our national economic focus.

Today's hearing is a continuation of Chairman Frank's efforts to coordinate and update the international economic development programs which fall within the jurisdiction of this subcommittee. A few weeks ago, we had a productive exploration of the Export-Import Bank. That hearing focused on the possibilities of opening up new, creative programs to facilitate the natural relationship between the economic development of Africa and African-American entrepreneurs in this country -- an issue which particularly interests me.

74-137 O - 94 - 3

Today we will hear about multilateral lending institutions, a huge contracting opportunity. It is estimated that the World Bank alone represents a $20 billion annual market for the procurement of goods and services.

Unfortunately, as testimony for this hearing illustrates, too often, U.S. export and international development programs are Europe-oriented. As with the Export-Import Bank, there are very few programs reaching out to Africa and other Third World countries. Additionally, export assistance programs in this country, often fall short of meeting the needs of minority-owned firms.

I look forward to this hearing. I also look forward to working with Chairman Frank and the other members of this subcommittee to merge the opportunities of multilateral lending institutions with small and medium sized businesses in this country.

JAMES A. TRAFICANT, JR.
17TH DISTRICT, OHIO

COMMITTEES
COMMITTEE ON PUBLIC WORKS AND TRANSPORTATION
CHAIRMAN, SUBCOMMITTEE ON PUBLIC BUILDINGS AND GROUNDS
SUBCOMMITTEE ON ECONOMIC DEVELOPMENT
SUBCOMMITTEE ON SURFACE TRANSPORTATION
COMMITTEE ON SCIENCE, SPACE, AND TECHNOLOGY
SUBCOMMITTEE ON SPACE
SELECT COMMITTEE ON NARCOTICS ABUSE AND CONTROL

Congress of the United States
House of Representatives
Washington, DC 20515-3517

2446 RAYBURN HOUSE OFFICE BUILDING
WASHINGTON, DC 20515
(202) 225-5261

11 OVERHILL ROAD
YOUNGSTOWN, OH 44512
(216) 788-2414

5555 YOUNGSTOWN-WARREN ROAD
SUITE 2685
NILES, OH 44446
(216) 652-5649

109 WEST 3RD STREET
EAST LIVERPOOL, OH 43920
(216) 385-5921

STATEMENT OF THE HONORABLE JAMES A. TRAFICANT, JR.
SUBCOMMITTEE ON INTERNATIONAL DEVELOPMENT, FINANCE, TRADE, AND MONETARY POLICY
NOVEMBER 18, 1993

Mr. Chairman and members of the committee, thank you for the opportunity to testify on the revised version of my bill, H.R. 2192. H.R. 2192 is a small business joint venture loan program with the newly independent states (N.I.S.) of the former Soviet Union.

As you know, I do not support foreign aid to any nation when our federal budget deficit is out of control and when we cannot afford to fund domestic programs. However, I recognize that unless there is stability in the world, the United States' federal budget deficit will continue to skyrocket and defense will continue to command a disproportionate amount of this nation's overall budget. I have introduced H.R. 2192 as a way to make federal expenditures on foreign aid more cost-effective and beneficial to American small businesses.

H.R. 2192 creates a loan program within the Import-Export Bank that will establish joint ventures between American small businesses and small businesses in the newly independent states. U.S. small businesses selected for participation in a joint venture must be more than 50 percent owned by U.S. citizens. In its present form, the bill authorizes $100 million for the overall program with a $100,000 maximum amount that can be loaned out for each joint venture.

It has been suggested that this program could serve as a model program in the Import-Export Bank, and could be expanded to encompass third world countries across the globe once the model has been proven successful. I agree and support this initiative. As a result, I have amended the bill to include small business joint ventures in both the NIS and Africa. The Import-Export Bank and the GAO (General Accounting Office) would then evaluate the program, and if the program is proven successful, it would be expanded to include other countries and continents at six month intervals.

A question has arisen on whether to appropriate new money for the program or use funding already in existence and earmark it for this program. I defer to the Chairman and the members of the committee, who know best, to determine the mechanism by which this program shall be funded.

This program isn't a hand-out, it's a hand-up. Instead of our government loaning money outright to foreign governments who may not have the resources to pay it back, my program would give American small businesses the opportunity to grow, and give NIS small businesses the opportunity to learn the American business know-how necessary to succeed and repay their loans.

My program is a responsible program. Under the bill, preference would be given to U.S. small businesses located in economically-depressed communities -- defined as communities which, relative to other communities in the United States, are depressed in terms of age of housing, the extent of poverty, the growth rate of per capita income, the extent of unemployment, job lag, or the extent of surplus labor. This provision would enable minority-owned small businesses located in both inner cities and rural areas to grow and expand into areas they otherwise could not due to lack of resources. Preference would also be given to loans that would be the most cost-effective, have the greatest likelihood of success, and most likely to benefit the participating U.S. small businesses and the

U.S. economy.

My legislation has numerous safeguards to protect American workers. First, it specifically prohibits the transfer of jobs from the United States. Absolutely no loans or joint ventures would be established with a U.S. small business which would transfer any business operations or activities that it has been carrying out in the United States to any location outside the United States. Second, all products, parts and components that are manufactured as a result of these joint ventures overseas cannot be reimported into the United States. U.S. products would not have to compete with these products made overseas, thereby protecting U.S. workers and U.S. jobs. Finally, my legislation includes numerous enforcement provisions to ensure that goods are not reimported into the United States. For example, all joint venture partners that produce goods for export must submit a notification specifying the foreign recipient of such exports, the identifying characteristics of such goods and the amount to be exported. This notification would be sent to the Commissioner of Customs.

The types of joint ventures I envision are ones in which the participating U.S. small business provides the management, accounting, marketing, training and other business expertise and the participating NIS and African small business provides the understanding of the local needs, conditions and resources needed by the joint venture.

Goods produced by the joint venture would be sold within the country of origin, or exported to any country other than the United States. In this way, the foreign small business is given an opportunity to learn American management and business expertise and the U.S. small business is given the opportunity to aggressively expand into a foreign market, developing the market to America's advantage.

In summary, my legislation places U.S. businesses in a good position to develop foreign markets for American products and skills. This increases the chance that, through these joint ventures, countries will learn to capitalize and democratize, and in doing so, will choose the U.S. as a trading partner. I urge your support for a responsible joint venture loan program that will provide much needed resources and skills to third world nations and empower American small businesses. I would be more than happy to address any concerns or answer any questions the members of the committee may have.

EMBARGOED FOR RELEASE
UPON DELIVERY
(APPROXIMATELY 2:00 p.m.)
TEXT AS PREPARED
FOR DELIVERY

Statement of Susan B. Levine
Deputy Assistant Secretary of the Treasury
International Development, Debt and Environment
Before the
Committee on Banking, Finance, and Urban Affairs Subcommittee on International Development, Finance, Trade and Monetary Policy
U.S. House of Representatives

November 18, 1993

Introduction

Mr. Chairman. Members of the Committee. I appreciate your invitation to testify on procurement opportunities for U.S. firms with the multilateral development banks. This is an extremely important issue for Treasury.

In testimony last spring, Secretary Bentsen made it clear that increasing business development and exports would be one of this Administration's most important objectives in the multilateral development banks. The U.S. already does well in this area, better as you might imagine, than any other G-7 country. Nevertheless, improving U.S. performance in this area is a key item on this Administration's agenda for change in the multilateral development banks.

Other agencies will clearly have major roles to play in this process. The Department of Commerce and the Trade and Development Agency are particularly valuable sources of support and technical expertise. I am pleased that representatives of these two agencies are here this afternoon.

We are working closely with both of these agencies to advance our commercial interests in the multilateral development banks. Our basic objectives are to assure that U.S. firms

(1) are made aware of business opportunities from the multilateral development banks as early as possible in the project cycle and

(2) that they have a full and fair chance to compete successfully with firms from other countries for this increasingly important business.

The International Context

We also need to look at this issue in a much broader context. Last year, the United States exported more than $619 billion in goods and services. Between 1987 and 1991, U.S. exports were the primary engine of growth in our domestic economy, accounting for 39 percent of the increase in our gross domestic product over that period.

As President Clinton has said, the United States cannot afford to retreat from the international economy. For our own selfish reasons, we need to help create a freer and more open international trading system within which the global economy can grow more rapidly. This approach will pay dividends on the home front. It is, in fact, the only way in which we can assure our nation's economic future and begin to create greater economic opportunities for our own people.

Our efforts to increase global growth are crucial at a time when economic growth has been negative or extremely slow in other industrial countries. Each percentage point increase in growth in other G-7 countries will result in more than $10 billion in U.S. exports each year. Under the Uruguay Round, lower tariff and non-tariff barriers to manufactured goods could increase world output by more than $5 trillion over the next ten years and U.S. output by more than $1 trillion.

Developing counties will also be affected. These countries have been the most rapidly expanding export market for U.S. merchandise exports over the past five years. U.S. exports to them went from just under $109 billion in 1987 to more than $181 billion in 1992. That was an increase of more than sixty-six percent, more than twice the rate of increase for our trade with other industrial countries. Under the Uruguay Round, we believe that full participation of developing counties in the global trading system could increase U.S. exports by an additional $200 billion over the next ten years.

The Reach of the Multilateral Development Banks

The Administration's approach to the multilateral development banks is part and parcel of our overall approach to international economic issues. The multilateral development banks play a central role in the international economic system. They encourage their borrowers to adopt policies that promote more rapid economic growth and more open trading practices. They have a financial reach that extends far beyond the capability of any single donor, including the United states.

This year, development bank loan commitments to developing countries will amount to more than $45 billion. Most of this money has come from funds that are raised in private capital markets and at no cost to the U.S. Government.

These loan commitments are a catalyst that increases the flow of private investment to developing countries. This further enhances the prospects for economic growth in those countries and creates even larger and more rapidly expanding demand for exports of U.S. goods and services.

Multilateral development bank loan commitments have gone to more than 100 borrowing countries in Asia, Africa, Latin America and in Central and Eastern Europe and the former Soviet Union. Many of the countries that have received these loans such as Argentina, Mexico and Pakistan have become important customers for U.S. exports. In many instances, the largest MDB borrowers are also the most important Export-Import Bank customers.

The multilateral development banks make loan commitments in many economic sectors. Their loans identify potential customers for a broad range of U.S. goods and services. The World Bank's sectoral distribution of lending for its most recent fiscal year presents a good example of the diversity of this market: agricultural and rural development $3.3 billion or 13.8 percent of total lending; transportation $3.2 billion or 13.4 percent; education $2.0 billion or 8.5 percent; urban development $2.0 billion or 8.5 percent; and population, health and nutrition $1.8 billion or 7.6 percent. This is a large market of great diversity that we cannot afford to stay out of.

Measuring U.S. Performance

As I indicated at the outset, the most recent statistical data that we have show that the United states is the most successful of the G-7 countries in terms of contracts awarded or disbursements made. The first chart at the end of my statement shows the U.S. at the top with an estimated $2.2 billion over the most recent fiscal years.

We do not have estimates for other countries in either the African Development Bank or the European Bank. However, in the other three banks for which we do have statistics, Germany and Japan come next after the United States, with each of them getting approximately $1.1 billion. Even in the Asian Development Bank, the U.S. received procurement of $210 million, marginally ahead of Japan with $206 million for calendar year 1992.

Also of note is how effective some of the developing countries have become at winning contracts on multilateral development bank projects. A second chart at the end of my statement ranks the top eleven recipients in each of the banks for which we have statistics. It shows India, Mexico and China in second, third and fourth places respectively in the World Bank with Germany, Japan and France in fifth, sixth and seventh places. The United Kingdom shows up in ninth place after Brazil.

Assessing the Impact

Behind the overall figures I have just cited lie a multitude of individual cases in which U.S. firms have won contract awards from MDB financed projects. These firms come from every part of the country. They include large international firms with extensive experience on major projects as well as small and medium-sized firms with more limited areas of expertise and experience. Taken together, these firms provide a very broad array of U.S. goods and services for MDB financed projects.

A few specific examples will show what I mean. McDermott International of New Orleans, Louisiana is a large firm with extensive international experience. In 1989, it led an international consortium which won a $407 million contract to develop the Oso off-shore oil condensate project in Nigeria. Of that amount, $265 million has come directly to the United States over the past three years to pay for compressors, generators, piping, steel tubing and other goods and services needed to complete the project.

The award of this contract has had a very positive impact on the economy of New Orleans where McDermott's international headquarters are located. We understand that four hundred people have worked on the contract there. Thirty other people have worked on site in Nigeria and still more were engaged in transporting barges and other equipment needed at the site.

The positive impact from the project was also felt in other parts of the country through the activities of subcontractors hired by McDermott. The compressors for the project came from Dresser Industries in New York. The turbine generators came from General Electric in California. Other important equipment came from Crowley Machinery in the State of Washington.

Other Large Disbursements

Other U.S. firms that have received relatively large disbursements on World bank projects during the past year include American Cast Iron Pipe from Birmingham, Alabama ($11 million); U.S. Chemical Resources from Tampa, Florida ($9.8 million); Caterpillar from Peoria, Illinois ($12.9 million); Cargill Incorporated from Minneapolis, Minnesota ($9.9 million); General Electric from New York ($10.5 million); Kellogg Overseas Corporation from Dallas, Texas ($17.3 million); and Sprint

International Communication Corporation from Reston, Virginia ($5.5 million).

A number of awards have also gone to consulting engineering firms that prepare the feasibility and prefeasibility studies which are the essential first steps in the project cycle. These firms also provide other important services such as preparation of final designs and project management and supervision.

A quick review of World Bank procurement data over the past year shows the following firms which have received disbursements on contracts of this type: Morrison-Knudsen of San Francisco, California; Stokes Engineering Company of Weston Connecticut; Deleuw Cather of Chicago, Illinois; Harza Engineering of Chicago, Illinois; Camp, Dresser and McKee of Boston, Massachusetts; Black and Veatch of Kansas City, Missouri; Louis Berger of East Orange, New Jersey; and Stone and Webster of New York.

U.S. accounting firms, management consulting firms, and other U.S. companies and organizations that provide specialized services have also done well in the MDBS. Last year, for example, the list of U.S. companies winning MDB contracts included Deloitte, Haskins, and Sells; Ernst and Young; Peat Marwick; Arthur D. Little; Booz, Allen, and Hamilton; and Price Waterhouse. U.S. universities have also done well. Last year's listing includes: the Midwest University Consortium, the University of Connecticut, Tulane University, Harvard University, Northeastern University, and the University of Wisconsin.

We do not have separate statistics on minority and women-owned firms, but last March, the African Development Bank's Board of Directors approved a project for $2.3 million which resulted in a contract being awarded to Theragen Incorporated of Capital Heights, Maryland. The contract is part of the bank's private sector development program. It supports a joint venture between Theragen and the Swaziland Investment Trust in the development of a pharmaceutical company in Swaziland. In recent years, two U.S. minority-owned investment banks -- Pryor McClendon and Courts and Doley Securities -- have served as co-managing underwriters for African Development Bank yankee bond offerings.

Financial services and the Environment

Let me turn now to the financial services industry, one with which I am quite familiar. Since 1989, the MDBs have raised more than $62 billion in public bond offerings. Of this amount, nearly $50 billion or 78 percent was either managed or co-managed by U.S. firms.

The environmental services industry is another key area which stands to derive significant benefits from the MDBs' greatly increased emphasis on environmental work. This work includes environmental impact assessment and monitoring and mitigation measures. U.S. firms have a strong technological lead vis-a-vis other countries in many important areas. It is one of the most promising areas for potential growth in the future. That is one of the benefits we expect to get from our participation in the Global Environment Facility.

MDB Reporting Systems and Procurement Policies

The procurement benefits I have just outlined are only the tip of the MDB iceberg. On average, MDB financing has represented about forty percent of the total costs of individual projects. The rest of the financing has come from other sources such as export promotion agencies and even more has come from the borrowing countries themselves. This additional financing is shown in the third chart at the end of my statement. It is directly related to MDB lending activity and, in many cases, gives U.S. suppliers an important opportunity for further business which is not reflected in the MDB reporting systems.

Other methodological issues arise with the reporting systems. MDB statistics do not always capture procurement benefits accruing to the United States. This is the case when U.S. firms bid through their foreign subsidiaries or as part of a joint venture or sub-contracting arrangement with foreign firms. For example, Caterpillar, one of the larger U.S. firms benefitting from MDB business, has indicated there are specific instances in which World Bank statistics did not fully capture the amount of business that had accrued to their firm.

We are continuing to work with the MDBs to improve the accuracy and comparability of information generated through their reporting systems. We also want to develop additional information on the importance of total project costs and subcontracting. Our overall view, however, is that the information reported to us by the MDBs is accurate and responsive to our needs.

There will always be some degree of distortion in any complex statistical process. From our point of view, it is most useful to focus on improving our outreach to the U.S. business community and on assuring that U.S. firms are treated fairly in the awarding of MDB contracts.

We believe that MDB procurement policies and practices must remain fair. Contracts above certain specific levels, which have varied among the MDBS, must continue to be awarded on the basis of international competitive bidding. This is a time-consuming and expensive process. It requires preparation of detailed and specific requests for tender, public announcements of the requests, and public opening of bids that are submitted.

But we believe that this system is necessary in order to maintain our competitive advantage. In several important respects, MDB bidding requirements are similar to those of the U.S. Government. Overall, we believe that the MDBs emphasis on international competitive bidding has served U.S. interests well.

Sometimes problems arise in the bidding process, and procedures are in place, both within the banks and within the U.S. Government, to deal with them. When we believe there is a possibility that U.S. firms have not been treated fairly, we have pursued those exceptions aggressively.

In some cases, we have been successful in reversing the awards of contracts and in bringing about a new round of international competitive bidding or in the cancellation of the loan amounts in question when the borrower is unwilling to make amends. For example, the World Bank cancelled $50 million of a loan to Turkey for highway construction when that country was unwilling to reverse an award.

Increasing U.S. Business

As I mentioned at the outset, we have a mandate to increase the commercial benefits of U.S. participation in the multilateral development banks. Our Executive Directors and Alternates are instructed to make business development and exports one of their highest priorities within the MDBS. We do not intend to treat this issue as a purely technical issue. In all of the banks, either the Director or the Alternate, with strong support from staff, will take primary responsibility for business development and procurement issues.

Within Treasury, we have created a new position: Assistant Director for Business Development and Exports. This position has been filled by a senior career official. He has overall responsibility within the office of Multilateral Development Banks for enhancing business outreach and for assuring that procurement policy issues are resolved. He will take a broad approach to these issues and seek to relate them more effectively to our other important policy objectives within the MDBS. We now have two professional staff members working on these types of issues at Treasury.

The Inter-Agency Process

We are also working to improve inter-agency support for MDB business matters. We rely heavily on the Commerce Department and the Trade and Development Agency in our efforts to improve U.S. commercial performance in the MDBS. Treasury has been a full participant in the Trade Promotion Coordination Committee.

Secretary Bentsen, Under-Secretary Summers, Assistant Secretary Shafer, and I have all participated in this process.

We are pleased with the results of that process as they relate to increasing our share of MDB business. Commerce has already assigned an additional commercial service officer to work with the office of the U.S. Executive Director at the African Development Bank and an additional environmental procurement officer is now in the office of the U.S. Executive Director at the Asian Development Bank. Additional commercial service staff are expected at the other banks in the near future. The concept of one-stop shopping for the MDBs has also been adopted at the Commerce Department in order to facilitate the assistance provided to U.S. business.

We are working closely with the Trade and Development Agency to support U.S. consulting engineers and other management consultants at the earliest stages of the project cycle. Both agencies-- Commerce and TDA-- will speak more to the specific details of their own programs in the MDBS. I simply wanted to emphasize how integral we believe their efforts are to the overall success of our program in the MDBs. We cannot succeed without their continuing and active involvement in encouraging a larger share of business for U.S. firms.

Enhancing Outreach to U.S. Business

Since the beginning of 1993, the multilateral development banks and the U.S. Government have sponsored or participated in more than 150 seminars or conferences designed to encourage participation of U.S. firms in the work of the multilateral development banks. Some of these seminars have been regularly scheduled monthly or quarterly meetings held by the MDBs to acquaint firms generally with the nature of their work and the possibilities for doing business. Others have been targeted at geographical areas within the United states or at MDB activities in certain borrowing countries or in specific economic sectors such as the environment or energy.

Earlier this month the Asian Development Bank concluded a series of seminars for U.S. firms in Boston, Milwaukee, Portland, and Honolulu. In June, a seminar on MDB work in the electric power sector was held here in Washington with the participation of approximately 150 U.S. firms including major contracting firms, engineers and consultants, private bankers and other financial services firms. Similar conferences have been held previously for the telecommunications, agricultural, and environmental sectors.

We believe these conferences and seminars have been very useful in promoting U.S. business. We plan to continue them in the future. We are very interested, however, in developing new mechanisms for involving the private sector more actively in our work at the MDBs and in refining our approach to different sectors of the U.S. business community.

For example, we are making preliminary plans now for a seminar targetted at small and medium-sized businesses with a special focus on minority and women-owned firms that we hope will take place in Chicago in the first quarter of next year. We believe that these types of firms that have been active in international activities may benefit from an approach that is specifically tailored to their concerns.

Conclusion

My statement today has focused on the commercial aspects of our national interest in the multilateral development banks. I do not want to leave you with the idea that we are in any way deemphasizing economic, political, strategic or humanitarian objectives that we have pursued in these international institutions. We will continue to work toward these and other important foreign policy goals that we have within the banks.

What we are doing within Treasury is putting much more emphasis on the commercial aspect of our participation in the banks. We intend to work more closely with other government agencies and with all members of the U.S. business community in this effort.

Frankly, in some cases, the most useful thing we can do is to get out of the way and let the other government agencies and U.S. business firms do the jobs they know how to do much better than we do. In other cases, we believe we will be able to provide a perspective or additional push that can help advance our commercial interests in the MDBs and we are very committed to doing that more effectively.

The final point I want to make is that we must also act to meet our financial obligations to the MDBS. At this time, we have arrearages in excess of $818 million. These arrearages interfere with the achievement of all our important policy objectives within the MDBS. This includes our long-term ability to generate greater commercial opportunities. It is important that we begin to reduce our arrearages over the next several years.

U.S. FIRMS GET LARGEST SHARE OF MDB G–7 PROCUREMENT *

World Bank/IDA: WBFY 1993 (to June 30, 1993)
(disbursements by address of payment)

United States	1393	8.0%
Germany	846	4.9%
Japan	846	4.9%
France	743	4.3%
U.K. (includes Hong Kong)	727	4.2%
Italy	386	2.2%
Canada	192	1.1%

International Finance Corporation
(private sector operations)
U.S. companies have participated as underwriters, company managers, equity investors, capital goods suppliers, lenders, technical partners, & providers of technical assistance.

Asian Development Bank Group: CY 1992
(contract awards by country of procurement/origin of goods)

United States	210	7.7%
Japan	206	7.5%
Germany	134	4.9%
U.K.	82	3.0%
Italy	72	2.6%
Canada	34	1.2%
France	21	0.8%

Inter–American Development Bank: CY 1992
(disbursements by origin of goods – convertible currency only)

United States	577	21.0%
Germany	133	4.8%
Japan	78	2.8%
Italy	65	2.4%
France	52	1.9%
United Kingdom	52	1.9%
Canada	45	1.6%

African Development Bank Group: CY 1992
(disbursements by address of payment)

$66 million (estimated) to U.S. addresses.

European Bank For Reconstruction & Development
(mixed information base)

Consulting: U.S. received 15 % of contract awards in CY 1992.
Merchant banking: U.S. companies have participated in 38% of merchant banking deals (6/91 to 9/93).

Development banking: no meaningful data available as yet.

* MDB Procurement: G–7 Shares of Total Procurement. Public data, for the most recent year available. (in US$ millions and in percent).

11/93

U.S. LARGEST -- BUT DEVELOPING COUNTRIES ARE IMPORTANT *

World Bank/IDA: WBFY 1993 (to June 30, 1993)
(disbursements by address of payment)

United States	1393	8.0%
India	1279	7.4%
Mexico	1132	6.5%
China (ex. Taiwan/ H.Kong)	1089	6.3%
Germany	846	4.9%
Japan	846	4.9%
France	743	4.3%
Brazil	815	4.7%
U.K. (includes Hong Kong)	727	4.2%
Indonesia	727	4.2%
Argentina	567	3.3%

Inter-American Development Bank: CY 1992
(disbursements by origin of goods – convertible currency only)

United States	577	21.0%
Brazil	303	11.0%
Mexico	259	9.4%
Chile	176	6.4%
Argentina	153	5.6%
Venezuela	139	5.1%
Germany	133	4.8%
Ecuador	118	4.3%
Colombia	90	3.3%
Japan	78	2.8%
Italy	65	2.4%

Asian Development Bank Group: CY 1992
(contract awards by country of procurement/origin of goods)

Indonesia	292	10.7%
Pakistan	246	9.0%
United States	210	7.7%
Japan	206	7.5%
Philippines	172	6.3%
India	171	6.2%
China	152	5.5%
Bangladesh	144	5.3%
Korea	135	4.9%
Germany	134	4.9%
U.K.	82	3.0%

African Development Bank Group: CY 1992
(disbursements by address of payment)

$66 million (estimated) to U.S. addresses.

European Bank For Reconstruction & Development
(mixed information base)

Consulting: U.S. received 15% of contract awards in CY 1992.
Merchant banking: U.S. companies have participated in 38% of merchant banking deals (6/91 – 9/93).

Development banking: no meaningful data available as yet.

* MDB Procurement: Relative Shares Of Top 11 – public data for the most recent year available.
(in US$ millions and in percent). (percentages are of total procurement and include project and adjustment lending). 11/93

U.S. BUSINESS OPPORTUNITIES GO BEYOND MDB SHARE OF PROJECT COSTS.

WB & IDA – Total Project Costs: WBFY 1993. *

(in US$ millions and in percent of total project costs)

	Total	Percent
All Projects		
Total Project Costs	$58,692.6	100%
IBRD/IDA	$23,695.9	40%
Local Contribution	$24,970.8	43%
Cofinancing	$10,025.9	17%
Other Multilateral	$3,194.8	5%
Bilateral	$3,654.5	6%
Export Credit	$1,218.1	2%
Private	$1,958.5	3%

* Financing plans at the time of Board Approval.
Additional cofinancing may appear during project implementation.

11/93

TESTIMONY OF

CHARLES A. FORD
ACTING DIRECTOR GENERAL
U.S. AND FOREIGN COMMERCIAL SERVICE
INTERNATIONAL TRADE ADMINISTRATION

BEFORE THE
COMMITTEE ON BANKING, FINANCE AND URBAN AFFAIRS
SUBCOMMITTEE ON INTERNATIONAL DEVELOPMENT, FINANCE, TRADE AND MONETARY POLICY
UNITED STATES HOUSE OF REPRESENTATIVES

NOVEMBER 18, 1993

INTRODUCTION

Mr. Chairman and members of the Subcommittee, thank you for inviting me here today. I appreciate this opportunity to appear before you to discuss the new and improved activities of the U.S. Department of Commerce in support of opportunities for U.S. business at the five multilateral development banks (MDBs).

Before I discuss this topic, I would like to sketch for you the framework within which we carry out this important task. The International Trade Administration (ITA) is the principal U.S. Government agency dedicated to assisting U.S. exporters. We are tasked with carrying out a number of activities designed to assist the U.S. business community -- including export counseling and marketing support; analyses of foreign market conditions and market access impediments; assessment of industry competitiveness; and development of marketing opportunities and sales representation through export promotion events and trade services. ITA carries out these activities through a team effort, bringing together the essential expertise needed to assist U.S. companies in foreign markets: country, industry and marketing specialists. These "export experts" work together in three units of ITA:

o Trade Development, which houses industry specialists, provides valuable information on trade and investment potential for specific products and industries. It is staffed by industry specialists that provide U.S. firms with a technical focal point in the Department for the promotion of their goods and services.

o International Economic Policy, which houses country desk officers, is an excellent source of information on trade and investment potential in specific countries. Every country in the world has an officer assigned to analyze market developments and commercial policy issues, and to serve as a focal point for market access initiatives.

o The U.S. and Foreign Commercial Service, comprised of the domestic and overseas commercial staff as well as a central export promotion unit, provides U.S. companies in every state and in 70 countries with marketing information, assistance and advocacy. Our District and Branch offices in the U.S. are an exporter's first stop for information on how to export. The commercial sections in our Embassies overseas are an important source of assistance on doing business in a particular country.

Mr. Chairman, let me return to the topic of our discussion here today: Department of Commerce support of U.S. private sector participation in MDB procurement. In order to maximize U.S.

company participation in MDB procurement it is vital that we determine the most appropriate role for the U.S. Government to play in this process. The specific needs of the private sector, which include (a) greater access to timely and substantive MDB project information, (b) enhanced outreach activities to expand the range of companies competing for MDB opportunities (particularly small and minority firms), and (c) active representation of companies by U.S. Government officials at the MDBs and throughout the borrowing member countries. These issues must be addressed aggressively if we are to continue to improve the success rates of U.S. companies bidding on MDB projects. In carrying out our program we have been, of course, working closely with our colleagues at Treasury and the U.S. Executive Directors, and will be expanding our activities with the Trade and Development Agency and other USG financing institutions.

RECENT ACTIVITIES

The Trade Promotion Coordinating Committee (TPCC), in fashioning a national export strategy, made several recommendations specifically regarding the MDBs. We in the Commerce Department are rapidly implementing these recommendations and increasing our focus on the MDBs throughout the domestic and overseas field networks. For example, in cooperation with our sister agencies, the Trade and Development Agency (TDA), the Overseas Private Investment Corporation (OPIC), Export-Import Bank (EXIM), Agency for International Development (AID), and the Small Business Administration (SBA), and other relevant components of the Trade Promotion Coordinating Committee (TPCC), we are putting in place focused, one-stop-shop offices to assist U.S. companies compete more effectively for business around the globe.

The U.S. and Foreign Commercial Service (US&FCS) has been tasked with organizing an aggressive outreach program to provide comprehensive counseling and expand our information dissemination on projects supported by the five MDBs. Trade Development will continue to monitor procurement policies and represent the commercial perspective in the interagency policy fora. The entire ITA network is prepared to carry forth a vigorous advocacy effort on behalf of American firms when necessary.

Placing the outreach responsibility within US&FCS, the marketing arm of ITA, responds to the TPCC mandate for a single, aggressive MDB promotion and business outreach office. Our US&FCS Office of Multilateral Development Bank Operations is that organization. This office will now develop the outreach program and provide support for all five MDBs.

A second TPCC recommendation is to increase liaison support for the U.S. Executive Directors to the MDBs. We are doing just that. Specifically, through the US-Asia Environmental Partnership, an expert on the environment and energy fields has been assigned to assist the US&FCS Senior Commercial Officer at the Asian Development Bank (ADB), and a second commercial officer has been placed in Abidjan to support the African Development Bank (AfDB) and run an expanded bilateral and regional promotion program. Commerce also expects to double the staff currently in place at the European Bank for Reconstruction and Development (EBRD), Inter-American Development Bank (IDB), and World Bank to further enhance their ability to support US business. The senior Commerce position in each institution will carry the rank of Senior Commercial Officer. We plan to have these personnel in place within the next six months.

All of the Commerce officers have been charged with four major activities: information/reporting, counseling, outreach, and advocacy, which I will discuss in more detail in a few moments.

A third TPCC recommendation is to integrate the role of MDBs into the broader USG export finance program agendas. At our Senior Commercial Officer's Conference in Miami we presented and discussed a unified program which addresses the role that each USG agency has in the financing arena. We defined the role of the overseas commercial staff in identifying and reporting on projects, and supporting American firms competing for MDB financing. The work of the overseas posts will be integrated into our domestic "one-stop-shop" portfolio. This conference on Latin America and the proposals which emanated therefrom will serve as a pilot in this area. We are also looking at the "one-stop-shop" concept as it applies to an ITA headquarters unit assisting firms in this area.

Finally, the TPCC recommended that we initiate a public information campaign to encourage U.S. firms to seek MDB financing. We are formulating plans now to expand our information dissemination through a variety of networks to increase our interface with the National Association of State Development Agencies (NASDA), World Trade Organizations, Chambers of Commerce, trade associations, and a host of other multipliers to carry the word through seminars, conferences, articles in trade publications, high visibility Ambassadors' Tours, trade shows and a wide variety of other means.

An important feature of the newly expanded program will be to dramatically increase the number of outreach programs conducted by Commerce Department staff at the IDB and the World Bank. These programs will build on those conducted around the country for the ADB, EBRD and AfDB and will spread the word on these two institutions to new customers throughout the United States.

The TPCC, the business community, members of Congress and the importance of MDB procurement to U.S. firms have all helped to focus our attention on the need to do more relative to the MDBs. We will do so by building on our experiences, as well as those of our colleagues in the U.S. Executive Director's offices and the Treasury Department. Let me briefly highlight for you our strategy and some of the successes which we have experienced to date.

INFORMATION/REPORTING

ITA has placed a high priority on increasing the flow of information on MDB project opportunities to the U.S. business community. By using the resources of the overseas and domestic network to collect and distribute this information through electronic and print media, we have improved the "early warning" so desired by business. Our specific sources of information collection and distribution are as follows:

o The US&FCS liaison officers gather and report information on MDB opportunities gathered from Bank publications, Bank staff, their colleagues throughout their area of operation, and other information sources.

o US&FCS and State Department commercial and economic officers also report on MDB opportunities that are uncovered in their individual markets.

All relevant early warning and in-depth international market insights (IMIs) on the MDBs are reported through the National Trade Data Bank (NTDB), the Economic Bulletin Board (EBB), the US&FCS Commercial Information Management System (CIMS), and a number of other sources.

o The EBB, the Department's on-line service, available by subscription, allows both timely market research and market specific information and trade opportunities such as foreign government tender announcements sent by commercial officers to be accessed by US companies within 24-48 hours of transmission from overseas. The EBB has over 4,500 subscribers. These subscribers consist of manufacturers, banks, service organizations, trade associations, and other multipliers. During FY 1993, there were over 5,100 reports entered into the EBB. While MDB information makes up only a small portion of the total information on the EBB it accounts for over 11% of total reports accessed. Clearly the subscribers are routinely accessing these early warning reports. In an exciting new development, the EBB is for the first time being made available to Internet subscribers. This will enable a large number of new users to access not just MDB related information but all trade related data that is contained on the EBB.

o Let me share an example from June of 1992, that demonstrates how the EBB can effectively disseminate MDB opportunities to the U.S. business community. A new-to-market company based in Charlotte, NC received information on a World Bank trade opportunity in Ecuador from the foreign government tenders program and proceeded to prepare a bid package. With the assistance of the Greensboro District Office and World Bank staff, the company was awarded a USD 3 million contract to supply energy control devices to Ecuador.

o The NTDB is a one-stop source for market research and international trade data collected from 16 federal government sources. The NTDB is available in over 900 Federal depository library sites, at each of the US&FCS district offices, as well as the majority of US&FCS overseas locations. Updated each month the NTDB is available on a subscription basis or in single disk sales. There are approximately 800 subscriptions and over 3,800 single sales this year. A series of detailed reports on the MDBs is included on the NTDB as well as market insight and alert reporting on specific project opportunities. Access to the NTDB enables district office and overseas staffs to actively counsel U.S. firms regarding the specific opportunities available at the MDBs.

o In addition to the EBB, all MDB tender announcements received from overseas posts are communicated to the Journal of Commerce and the Commerce Business Daily.

o US&FCS also maintains an excellent working relationship with ITA's Eastern Europe Business Information Center (EEBIC) and the Business Information Service for the Newly Independent States (BISNIS). These information centers serve as effective multipliers for the dissemination of MDB project information and for the recruitment of outreach programs. As we initiate an expanded outreach program for the IDB, we plan to utilize the working relationship the IDB liaison officer has established with the Latin American Business Development Center to perform these same functions in this important region. The TPCC recommended that the Trade Information Center be used as the single TPCC-wide information office that will coordinate existing specialized nonagricultural export information offices. We feel this would be an extremely effective mechanism for integrating MDB outreach and information programs into the overall initiatives of the Commerce Department and other relevant USG agencies.

COUNSELING ACTIVITIES

Our liaison officers have all established an active and effective counseling program to ensure that interested U.S. companies are provided with the specific information that will enable them to pursue and win MDB financed opportunities. During the last two years, the number of U.S. companies contacting the liaison officers via fax, phone, and visits to their MDB offices has increased at an incredible rate. For example, the ADB liaison officer has noted an increase of 200% in the number of visitors seeking procurement assistance in Manila and a 300% increase in the number of letter and fax requests for information. Similar increases have been reported by the AfDB and EBRD liaison officers. Visitors to the Bank liaison officers range from small and medium sized firms seeking a special niche in MDB financed projects to major manufacturing companies and large design, engineering and construction firms seeking specialized counseling and representation. In many cases, the liaison officers are able to arrange special briefings with local officials and MDB staff members thus enabling U.S. firms to familiarize decision makers with their specific expertise.

Additional counseling activities are undertaken by Washington based support staff, ITA country and industry specialists, and trade specialists throughout the US&FCS domestic offices. These individuals have MDB information on-hand and have direct links to the officers overseas enabling them to provide U.S. companies with the information they require to begin making rational and intelligent decisions about pursuing MDB financed projects.

OUTREACH PROGRAMS

Each of the MDB liaison officers will conduct a vigorous and innovative outreach program to convey MDB related information directly to groups of interested U.S. companies. In the last two years, the liaison officers have conducted more than 75 outreach programs in 25 U.S. cities reaching over 5000 business persons. Our three overseas based officers have also been involved in at least 30 programs in 19 countries throughout their respective regions of responsibility. The programs conducted were quite varied and attempted to reach different types of audiences ranging from small and medium sized companies to the large multinationals that already have a significant presence in many of these emerging markets. For example:

o The Mid-America Committee and the Department of Commerce sponsored an Ambassador's Tour in April/May of 1993. The Alternate U.S. Executive Director to the World Bank and the EBRD liaison officer participated in this multi-city program featuring the U.S. Ambassadors to four Eastern European countries as well as five US&FCS Senior Commercial Officers and representatives from other USG agencies such as OPIC, TDA, and the Export Import Bank. This highly successful program introduced over 500 U.S. business people to the trade opportunities in this growing market and the programs offered by the various government agencies to assist companies in tapping this market. The EBRD and World Bank contacts were an important component of this program and provided substantive information on the lending programs and assistance available through these institutions.

o MDB officers will be participating in the US-ASEAN Council sponsored Ambassadors' Tour during 1994 as well as an Ambassadors' Tour focusing on Russia and the NIS next summer.

o The AfDB liaison officer is conducting a series of seminar programs focusing on specific industry sectors where U.S. firms are highly competitive and which receive large amounts of Bank project lending. This program enables U.S. companies to have direct, face-to-face contact with important AfDB and local government contacts.

o Seminars focusing on "How to Do Business" with the MDBs have been very successful. Programs on all five MDBs have been equally successful whether they focus solely on a specific Bank or take advantage of representatives of other USG agencies such as the Trade and Development Agency or MDB staff members to complement the discussion and provide additional insights to U.S. companies. The continued interest in these programs is evidenced by two recent programs in Washington focused on the EBRD and TDA which were attended by over 150 firms.

o A success from a recent program in San Francisco demonstrates the potential of the seminar program. Discussions during the program led a California company to submit a USD 5 million proposal to the EBRD. Follow on assistance from the EBRD officer including assistance with the company's proposal and negotiating on behalf of the company has led to the project being cleared by the EBRD's operation committee. Of course the project must await discussion and approval by the EBRD Board of Directors.

ADVOCACY/REPRESENTATION

Representing the interests of U.S. firms directly to MDB staff is one of the more critical functions performed by the liaison officers. The ability not only to approach Bank staff on behalf of U.S. company interests but also to effectively mobilize the resources of local US&FCS commercial officers, State Department economic officers, and Ambassadors has been a key to U.S. success on many occasions.

o An excellent example of this culminated in the successful intervention on behalf of two U.S. companies, one based in Massachusetts and the other in Illinois, bidding on a USD 3 million ADB project to develop a stock exchange in the Philippines. Throughout 1992 and early 1993, the ADB liaison officer made numerous requests of ADB staff to review the bid package prepared by the U.S. companies. The ADB liaison was able to encourage the U.S. Ambassador to the Philippines to intervene with ADB officials on behalf of the companies and to arrange meetings to negotiate fine points of the proposed project.

Follow up work was done during the US-ASEAN Ambassadors' Tour and eventually the firms won the contract, winning out over competition from Canada, the UK, and Taiwan.

o Recently, a dispute was resolved in favor of a U.S. company on a contract award from the World Bank. Despite the fact that the evaluation committee concluded that a hydroelectric project design contract should be awarded to a New York based firm, senior Malawi government officials requested the World Bank confirm the award to a German firm. The Department's World Bank liaison officer interceded with World Bank officials thereby assuring that the U.S. firm, which had the most competitive bid, was awarded this USD 21 million contract.

o Based on the procurement statistics provided by my colleague from Treasury, it is clear that U.S. firms have enjoyed success competing for MDB opportunities. A few additional examples of U.S. wins at the MDBs follow: a USD 26 million ADB contract for the design and construction of an airport in Mongolia was awarded to a Virginia firm, a USD 34.5 million AfDB contract to build a railroad connecting Tanzania and Zambia was awarded to two New York firms, and a USD 18 million IDB contract for the sale of cranes to Mexico was awarded to an Alabama firm.

A final and important component of the advocacy/dispute resolution aspect of the MDB procurement liaison officer job is helping to assure that the MDBs manage transparent and competitive procurement systems. Here the MDB liaison officers contribute their technical expertise and participate in the formulation of U.S. positions on MDB procurement policies and procedure.

Commerce is also an active participant in the Working Group on Multilateral Aid (WGMA), an interagency group chaired by Treasury, that ensures that MDB projects assist a country's development and are consistent with U.S. economic, national security, and foreign policy objectives. Commerce will continue to work closely with Treasury on this important policy function.

COMMERCE DEPARTMENT INITIATIVES FOR 1994

Our 1994 program will incorporate all the elements I have described and build upon the activities and the network we have established.

We will continue to introduce new and innovative outreach program concepts that will further expand the existing clientele of the MDBs. For example, we plan to utilize privately organized trade shows in industry sectors of special importance to the MDBs such as the Power Generation and hazardous materials shows. We will utilize State and local organizations such as the Pennsylvania Department of Commerce Small and Minority Affairs Office to assure that we reach all segments of the business community. The initiation of reverse trade missions matching key U.S. industries with specific country markets with significant MDB lending will bring foreign government decision makers to the United States to meet directly with U.S. industry leaders that are able to meet the special needs of these countries. Programs of this type will be conducted with the assistance of other USG agencies such as the Trade and Development Agency and the Overseas Private Investment Corporation.

The Commerce office at each of the five MDBs will be headed by a Senior Commercial Officer. These officers will fully participate in the regional Senior Commercial Officer and Business Outlook programs and will be involved in training their country based colleagues in the intricacies of MDB financing. Valuable contacts with interested U.S. companies will also be developed.

CONCLUSION

Mr. Chairman, once again I thank you for the opportunity to share with you and your colleagues the progress we have made and our plans for the future. I look forward to working with each of you to assure the best possible support for American business.

U.S. TRADE AND DEVELOPMENT AGENCY

Testimony of Barbara R. Bradford

Regional Director
U.S. Trade and Development Agency

Before the
House Banking Committee
Subcommittee for International Affairs

on
Multilateral Development Bank Procurement

November 18, 1993

Thank you for the opportunity to appear before the Subcommittee. The Trade and Development Agency does not usually testify before this committee, so we are especially pleased to be here today to discuss multilateral development bank procurement.

The U.S. Trade and Development Agency, or TDA, is a commercially-oriented foreign assistance agency. TDA relates closely to the Departments of State and Commerce in their missions to promote U.S. foreign policy goals in developing countries, as well as to promote U.S. exports.

TDA strongly supports the President's efforts to increase U.S. exports from the United States, and TDA is an active participant in the Trade Promotion Coordinating Committee, which was organized to support these efforts.

TDA is appearing before the Subcommittee today in its role as a U.S. agency which is actively involved in helping U.S. firms to increase

Room 309 SA-16, Washington, D.C. 20523-1602
Telephone (703) 875-4357 • Fax (703) 875-4009

their share of procurement from the multilateral development banks (or MDBs).

TDA uses its funds to position U.S. firms to sell goods and services to infrastructure and industrial projects in the developing world. TDA does this primarily by getting involved in these major projects at the drawing board stage when the ante is low. TDA often funds feasibility studies for MDB-financed projects. These studies are carried out by U.S. engineering and consulting firms with the objective of directing procurement toward U.S. companies when the projects move off the drawing board and into the implementation stage. For example, in 1989, TDA funded a feasibility study in Turkey for a large education project involving the procurement of millions of dollars of computers and peripheral equipment. U.S. firms exported over $130 million of equipment to this project under procurement financed by the World Bank.

TDA also funds other activities, such as technical symposia and training, in situations where it believes these activities can help U.S. firms win contracts overseas.

Another TDA activity has been to make occasional grants to multilateral development banks in order to encourage the use of U.S. consultants in helping the banks to appraise potential projects. These grants are often referred to as "trust funds," although TDA's grants might better be looked upon as ongoing experiments while the United States considers the significant issues surrounding an official policy on trust funds.

Many of our competitor nations have trust funds at the MDBs. They are used in a variety of ways to achieve numerous goals. There is not just one type of trust fund which automatically achieves a higher proportion of MDB procurement for its donor nation. The effective use of a trust fund depends more on how it is administered than the amount of money in it.

The World Bank represents a $20 billion annual market for the procurement of goods and services. A look at the annual report of the World Bank shows that U.S. firms obtain a relatively small share of the category of procurement entitled "equipment." TDA's goal is to increase the U.S. share in this category.

The multilateral development banks are complex organizations that require a thorough and sophisticated approach in order to be effective when it comes time to compete for bank procurement. TDA administers its funds to provide U.S. firms with early information on MDB projects to help them compete. TDA's trust funds represent a significant leveraging mechanism involving a relatively small sum of money that has a significant effect on U.S. exports. Preliminary figures provided by the banks themselves show the funds provide between $40 and $178 in exports for every dollar TDA spends. In large part, this success is based on the effective relationships TDA has forged with MDB staff, and its ability to gain early project information on MDB projects and deliver it to U.S. firms.

TDA has five trust funds at four of the multilateral development banks. These trust funds are located at the World Bank; at the International Finance Corporation, which is the private sector arm of the World Bank; at the European Bank for Reconstruction and Development in London; and at the African Development Bank in Abidjan, Ivory Coast. Specifically, TDA has two trust funds at the World Bank, one a general fund and the other focused on Africa.

The first of TDA's five trust funds was established at the African Development Bank in 1986. Since 1986, TDA has put a total of $11,631,000 into the five trust funds. The larger and more active of the funds have been those at the World Bank, and that Bank has been TDA's primary focus over the past year.

I will use the example of the World Bank to illustrate how the trust funds work. In 1989, TDA made a grant of $500,000 to the World Bank to establish a fund to pay for U.S. consultants to appraise projects in selected countries. TDA retains final approval over how each penny of that money is spent. The Bank staff, in preparing a project, will request the use of a U.S. consultant to help in the formulation of the project. The Bank requests permission from TDA to use trust fund money to pay for the consultant. TDA reviews the Bank's description of what the U.S. consultant would do, and analyzes the Bank's proposal according to TDA's usual criteria: Does the project represent the potential for a significant amount of U.S. exports? Is the United States competitive in the sector? Is there likely to be foreign competition for U.S. firms in this project? On the basis of this review, TDA either approves or disapproves the use of its trust fund for the purpose proposed by the Bank. TDA's decision on whether or not to use the fund is final.

In cases where use of a U.S. consultant is approved, TDA tracks the progress of the consultant and the project. The consultant is debriefed by TDA once the work for the Bank is concluded. U.S. firms have indicated that the information gained from this debriefing is useful in their efforts to determine which MDB procurements to pursue. TDA publishes the information in its newsletter for U.S. firms, the TDA *Bi-Weekly*. TDA backs up this information with training for U.S. firms on how to compete and win World Bank procurement awards. TDA can also provide additional funds to a World Bank project, for example, funding the feasibility study, in cases where we believe that additional U.S. involvement in the development of the project will significantly increase the chances that U.S. goods and services will be used in the project.

TDA has developed an effective program through its trust funds to assist U.S. firms in their efforts to succeed in the lucrative market that the banks represent. It appears the effectiveness of the trust funds is not only based upon the amount of money in them, but also on developing effective working relationships with the banks, being involved in determining which projects the money will be used for, tracking those projects as they develop, and providing early information about them to U.S. firms. TDA has gained the experience and developed the relationships and mechanisms necessary to be effective.

Thank you for your time and attention to this important matter. I will be happy to answer any questions you may have.

Testimony offered by

Manuel A. Medina

Cape Verdean-American Import/Export, Inc.,
8 South Street, New Bedford, Massachusetts 02740

before the Subcommittee on International Development,
Finance, Trade and Monetary Policy
U.S. House of Representatives

November 18, 1993

My family-owned shipping company operates the only scheduled ocean freight service between the USA and the Cape Verde Islands, West Africa. For over one hundred years there has been a commercial sea link between southeastern New England and these islands. Hundreds of small businessmen have been involved in this trade over the years. Since mid-1988 the company has moved over 888,000 cubic feet of cargo to West Africa and generated in excess of $2.1 million dollars in documented business in the greater New Bedford area. At the present time we employ thirty people. Regardless of the declining industrial base and the continuing hard times confronting our region, our Cape Verdean-American clients regard our service as nothing short of critical. With a lot of hustle on our part my company can always generate sufficient cargo to justify scheduling a shipment. And yet we profoundly understand that our business will never grow so long as we are dependent on immigrant cargo. We have always known that in order to grow our company must be exporting American manufactured goods to foreign buyers.

As a small minority firm we are encouraged by all of the talk out of Washington about the central role of export promotion in the economic recovery plans of the Clinton Administration. The primary beneficiaries of these export promotion measures will be small manufacturing companies and distributors of unique services and products. Shipping companies like mine will be secondary beneficiaries of any sustained expansion in the export sector.

The City of New Bedford is an economically depressed area which in spite of its excellent port and existing export capabilities has been living on a hand-to-mouth basis for years. About 120 years ago New Bedford was sold down the river by the owners of the whale oil industry. Fifty years ago the owners of the textile industry abruptly moved South in hot pursuit of cheap labor. Today everyone is worried about threats to move the remaining manufacturing jobs even further to the South. It is ironic that these hearings are taking place at the same time that the USA is debating trade agreements which many people profoundly believe will threaten their jobs. Workers in cities like New

Bedford simply do not trust all of this talk about what will get better in the next generation if only we make sacrifices today. Its really not about ideology its about keeping the jobs we have and understand.

With all of the talk about exports there seems to be a major gap between the pronouncements of the government and concrete demonstrations of real interest in manufacturing goods for export and simultaneously aggressively backing up the efforts of private business people to open up foreign markets. If the US is serious about expanding exports why do we still have to wrestle through so much red tape in order to get information about financing exports? What do we have to do to get our Embassies behind our efforts to introduce US products and get trading relationships off the ground no matter how small they may appear to be?

Our President talks about expansion in the export business as part of the defense of America's permanent economic interests and yet we still don't seem to be using the resources of small companies like mine to really develop this export capability. It in not for lack of resources that our government doesn't seem to be helping small companies in the export business. I think it has something to do with how our government thinks about the potential of small companies. I believe it has to do with the lack of creativity to use the resources America has and determination to back up the individuals and private companies who put themselves on the line trying to make it in the export business. In the case of small shipping companies so many of our problems are related to financing for growth. Our government maintains a huge "moth ball fleet" of vessels many of which are ideally suited for opening up trade to small ports around the world. And believe it or not it would take an Executive Order of the President to allow one of these rusting cargo vessels to be leased by a US shipping company.

At our end and at the base there are problems with how matters are perceived. The very self perception of the people and the way we evaluate the economic resources of our city must be fundamentally changed if we are to risk trusting our government to deliver on the promises of export promotion and economic growth.

The expansion in export sales is being used as an example by the Administration as a necessary condition for any permanent economic turn around for the country. If this is the case then how is it that the government has done so little to develop the export sector in cities like New Bedford?

New Bedford has centuries-old cultural attachments to many parts of the world which are now poised for economic growth. The city abounds with abandoned but usable manufacturing space and a labor force still driven by a traditional work ethic.

The other problem perception is that New Bedford is so far out of the information loop after being the victim of double digit unemployment for so long that local business people don't see any connection between themselves and all of this talk about exports. And the situation with minority firms is even worse. Frankly, people are so beaten down that they don't believe that these federal export programs have anything to do with us.

How can small companies be expected to invest their limited capital to learn how to access the accountants, lawyers, commercial bankers, the Department of Commerce information and other technical assistance on the basis of government rhetoric about export expansion? Whenever my company has discovered a potentially profitable new venture we invariably lose valuable time in our efforts to secure financing. So often by the time we find the financing another larger firm has taken advantage of our research and investment of time. Many of the opportunities for breaking into export sales of which we are aware have been lost to us because of the way EEC and other trading blocs take care of their own. In our case, many of the projects we want to supply receive their funding through EEC countries foreign assistance programs and have the requirement that only EEC goods be procured. We have invested our energies to prepare bids for supplying foreign projects only to discover that the specifications have been pre-approved. We actually have been in situations where when equality of bids is achieved and preference is still automatically given to those companies of EEC countries or other trading blocs.

In the West Africa region we see imports from suppliers in Portugal, France, Brazil and other countries. The quality of these manufactured goods is generally inferior to US made products. What stops us from aggressively getting into an export business is financing and a lack of up to date market information.

Workers in cities like ours seem to be victims of the "new language" coming out of the national government. For us all of the talk about "retraining for a service economy" is very futuristic. Until the government begins to help private business produce real jobs people in my city will have problems believing that these federal programs are for people like us. To really achieve anything of lasting value the government needs to institute hand-to-hand outreach programs which put good managers together with small groups of people who are then systematically helped to take advantage of situations and programs as they occur. Federal programs need to be designed from the bottom up if they are ever to achieve any sustainable impact and growth in the New Bedfords of America.

I do not want to overstate the importance of small firms in the overall economic scheme of things but I firmly believe that all of the people-to-people negotiations involved in buying and selling in an open market by small American and foreign private companies plays a major role in the on-going democratization process to which our country is committed. I do not believe we can have one without the other.

In closing, Congressman Frank, I would like to state that since you became our representative every sector in our city has been getting lots attention. People, organizations, unions and politicians who are not accustomed to talking with one another are constantly finding themselves not only in the same room together but actually invited to sit at the negotiating table with you. This is no small achievement and we are appreciative. Expectations have been raised. But I believe that the problems in New Bedford are of such depth and of such long standing that they are really beyond what a Congressional office can handle. I hope your Subcommittee will seize this opportunity to make the promise of growth in the export sector come true for New Bedford so that we may be able to begin to economically heal ourselves.

American Consulting Engineers Council
1015 Fifteenth Street, N.W., Washington, D.C. 20005
202-347-7474
FAX: 202-898-0068

PROCUREMENT AND MULTILATERAL DEVELOPMENT

Testimony of

ROBERT C. ULRICH

Before the

THE HOUSE COMMITTEE ON BANKING, FINANCE, AND URBAN AFFAIRS, SUBCOMMITTEE ON INTERNATIONAL DEVELOPMENT, FINANCE, TRADE AND MONETARY POLICY

On Behalf Of

THE AMERICAN CONSULTING ENGINEERS COUNCIL

November 18, 1993

INTRODUCTION

Good Afternoon Mr. Chairman and Distinguished Members of the Committee:

My name is Robert Ulrich, Vice President and Group Marketing Manager, Parsons Brinckerhoff International, a 108 year old engineering firm. I am here representing the American Consulting Engineers Council (ACEC) and I would like to thank members of the committee for this opportunity and to speak on behalf of U.S. participation in Multilateral Development Bank funded projects.

ACEC, a federation of fifty-one (51) state and regional councils, is a national association representing 4,500 private practice consulting engineering firms employing over 180,000 engineers, scientists, technicians and other support personnel who annually design over $100 billion in constructed public works and private industry facilities. With the architects, constructors and contractors, we account for approximately 15% of the United States' Gross National Product (GNP). According to *Engineering News Record* magazine, the U.S. design industry alone accounted for $6.1 billion in U.S. exports in 1992.

ACEC's member firms have worked with the MDBs for decades and carved out markets for U.S. services and goods in 168 countries. U.S. engineers have conducted feasibility studies, design and supervision of construction water and sewerage systems, power plants, roads, bridges, sea ports and airports as well as other infrastructure facilities. When development assistance is used for infrastructure projects, **everybody wins**. The developing countries get the infrastructure they desperately need and Americans get jobs -- jobs in the foreign countries, jobs in the home offices and jobs in the plants that supply the required goods and equipment which successfully implement and sustain those development projects.

U.S. firms also receive additional benefits by working overseas - prestige and the ability to make lasting business contacts within a foreign country. Since U.S. firms usually joint venture with a local firm, a significant amount of technology transfer also occurs during the course of a project's implementation. This ensures that local firms are exposed to U.S. training and taught the requisite program management techniques with regard to the delivery of engineering services. They are learning from the best in the world because our firms are on the cutting edge of new technology.

Two years ago, ACEC was invited by Congress to identify those areas of procurement that could use improvement. Soon afterwards, Congressmen Bereuter and Gejdenson attached amendments (under Title V) to last years OPIC Reauthorization Bill that addressed the problems raised in our testimony. The amendments established technical assistance funds at the MDBs; expanded the procurement staff at the U.S. Executive Directors' Offices; and called for greater accessibility to procurement information and internal bank documents.

Today, we understand that a reference room will soon open that provides project information and documents to the industry. This information delivers the needed input to our planning and pursuit of procurement opportunities. The increase in procurement staff has not yet occurred but we continue to believe that we will see new people in those offices in the very near future.

Turning to trust funds, the Trade and Development Agency (TDA) has established technical assistance funds at the MDBs. But these funds need to be capitalized at a higher level. It is simply an issue of improving the return on our existing investment. We have established a working relationship between our industry and the U.S. Department of Treasury. Through the efforts of Nelson Coar, International Economist at the Treasury Department, a spirit of cooperation and good will has developed on trade issues that concern our industry.

Yet, we need only to look at the Asian Development Bank (ADB) to see the success of MDB investment. After a substantial period of investment in infrastructure and small industry, the region today boasts the highest economic growth rates in the world. More importantly, we are also witnessing the growth of democracy. Regardless of the MDB's financial importance to our industry, each of the MDB's have proven themselves to be critical factors to achieving sustainable growth in developing countries. This means bigger markets for U.S. goods and services. In the big picture, the MDB's investments throughout the world should be lauded.

We thank the subcommittee, its staff, and particularly Congressman Bereuter, for your concern and commitment to the promotion of service industry exports. According to the Department of Commerce which has also been helpful to us, the U.S. has a trade surplus of $18 billion this year in the services' sector. This figure supports our premise that if we all work together, we can compete with **any country** in the global market.

I would like to make three fundamental points which will serve to highlight the importance and effectiveness of the MDB's to industry, as well as to overall U.S. economic interests.

-- First, I would like to explain how the U.S. engineering industry **drives trade** by specifying other U.S. services and goods;

-- Secondly, I would like to talk about the importance of **increasing** the level of U.S. trust funds;

-- and finally, I will touch on what we believe should be the necessary **support elements** of the U.S. and Foreign Commercial Service personnel who are employed by the U.S. offices at these banks.

I. HOW U.S. ENGINEERING DRIVES EXPORTS

The main purpose of the MDB's is to create and sustain economic stability in developing countries. As part of that overarching process, the MDBs finance infrastructure projects which help support that stability. **Subsequently, those projects create markets for U.S. firms in those developing countries**. The potential to export is great and affects a variety of different areas -- power, telecommunications, environment, education, and transportation. We know it is difficult during these budget constrained times to talk about foreign assistance programs, **but let me make it clear that what I am talking about today is not foreign assistance**, but rather a comprehensive strategy on how to level the playing field for U.S. firms pursuing overseas work in the MDB market place. What I am speaking about plain and simple is export promotion. ACEC believes that Americans would more enthusiastically support foreign assistance if they knew that **MDB financed projects provide a win - win situation** for the U.S and developing countries alike. MDB funded projects:

1. provide developing countries with the means to implement long-term solutions to their environmental and infrastructure needs while promoting sustainable development through training and education;

2. encourage support for emerging democracies by enhancing economic stability in lesser developed and newly-industrialized countries;

3. assist U.S exporters in carving out overseas markets for U.S. services and goods;

4. produce jobs for Americans here at home and promote the use of U.S. technologies overseas;

5. improve the U.S. balance of trade and;

6. enhance local engineering capabilities through joint ventures and technology transfer.

The engineering community plays a significant role in increasing the volume of U.S. exports around the world. **Engineering services are the "opening wedge" of the entire export process**. The fact is, is that when you commit to the engineering of a project, you are making the first hard commitment to the project process. That commitment incorporates the development of standards and specifications which will dictate the ability of U.S. suppliers and manufacturers to compete for "follow on" contracts.

Because engineering firms are responsible for project design, they are also responsible for developing the technical specifications for further equipment and processes required for construction. These have included equipment and goods needed for the construction of wastewater treatment plants, potable water systems, irrigation, roads, airports and seaports, cleanup of hazardous waste, communications, as well as other vital infrastructure projects. Additionally, follow on services for U.S. firms are also created in the form of education programs as well as start-up and training opportunities. These specifications provide an opening wedge for additional U.S. exports to the region, in turn, increasing the competitiveness of U.S. firms and their products around the globe.

Our international competition is well aware of this "opening wedge" relationship between engineering services and how they relate to follow on exports. The Japanese, Germans, and French among others are aggressively competing with our firms, causing the U.S. share of the international construction market to decline over the past several years. By increasing the share of the MDB projects awarded to U.S. engineering firms, the U.S. economy prospers from an increased share of the international construction market.

II. THE IMPORTANCE OF TRUST FUNDS

The U.S. could vastly increase its market share if U.S. trust funds financed small, but early portions of capital projects. In order for the U.S. firms to capture a greater portion of the MDB market, it must increase the levels of these trust funds (supplemental to that of the Trade and Development Agency) and they must be devoted specifically to engineering and architectural services. **Trusts give U.S. firms the first shot at a major project**. We can compete more effectively with our foreign competition because trusts finance the initial portion of the project, which gives U.S. firms higher visibility with the foreign government when the project moves into its implementation phase. Simply put, trust funds enhance a U.S. firm's chances at winning projects.

Trust funds are nothing more than an insurance policy. For example the U.S. owns 10% of the share of the European Bank for Reconstruction and Development (EBRD). We are the largest single country shareholder of the EBRD. But, when it comes to procurement of engineering services, we do little insure our overseas investment in the Bank. U.S. TDA provides $1.1 million in trust funds for U.S. firms to perform project studies. Conversely, not only do the member nations of the European Community collectively provide roughly some $40 million dollars with which to draw upon in the form of trusts, but certain countries have also established **individual trusts** in that bank, reserved specifically for their design firms to bid on projects. Competitor nations recognize the importance of having trust funds to assure getting their fair share of projects.

In the case of my own firm, Parsons Brinckerhoff has been shortlisted for technical assignments on three different occasions by the EBRD. On each occasion, we found that French or German competitors have won the job. Why ? - Trust funds. **Trust funds help to promote and support national interests**. Quite simply, we need more trust funds, and more U.S. funding to obtain a larger share of the EBRD market for project design.

For example, in 1993 the World Bank co-financed 118 projects at a cost of 11 billion dollars. Other nations co-financed an additional 7.7 billion dollars which drove some 35.5 billion dollars in projects. When you hear those numbers, you should realize how important it is for the U.S. to participate in these procurements on an equal footing with our competitors.

III. SUPPORT MECHANISMS

The Offices of the U.S. Executive Directors have one function: to look after the interests of the United States. It is through these offices that export promotion for U.S. products and services takes place. In order to perform this task effectively, the U.S. Executive Directors should be stationed, during their tenure, in the city in which the MDB is located. The U.S. Foreign and Commercial Service and its staff support the MDBs' U.S. Executive Directors. These positions are critical to the U.S. private sector because they represent a vital link between business and government. **But it is time we look at this part of the process as the rest of the world does -- as a business.** And that is exactly what it is. The U.S. Government can and should play a role in enhancing the export capabilities of the private sector and therefore the people that staff those positions need to be of the caliber to be a linchpin in this critical process.

The key to the successful pursuit of an MDB financed project is accurate and timely information as well as the ability of the foreign and commercial service to be proactive rather than reactive. Increased staffing levels for procurement specialists in the U.S. Executive Directors' Offices will improve the quality and quantity of information needed to pursue overseas opportunities, it will also serve to protect U.S. interests and support the MDBs in contract issues. We have asked for this to stay competitive and we have found that the Executive Directors from other countries routinely provide this information to their engineering firms. We know this because some of our firms are getting their information through their foreign subsidiaries.

ACEC also believes that U.S. personnel who staff positions at the banks should be trained at a level that is consistent throughout the entire system. They should have a solid business background and/or have worked extensively with the private sector in helping them identify, support and advocate the use of U.S. firms in international development projects. Furthermore, all new hires should be sufficiently trained in specific targeted market sectors of developing countries which are growing at a rapid rate in order to maximize the export of additional follow on goods and services. The council is doing its part as well. Each year we educate over 100 Foreign Commercial Service personnel on what consulting engineers do and the information they need to be competitive overseas.

CONCLUSION

ACEC has been leading the effort in the U.S. Engineering and Construction industries to support the Administration's effort to increase exports. ACEC believes that the consulting engineering industry and the Clinton Administration's goals of job creation, the promotion of U.S. exports and the revitalization of the American economy are not only consistent, but interdependent. The U.S. also demonstrates global leadership when it combines these objectives with sound, long term development policies using institutions such as the MDBs to accomplish those ends and which serve to improve the living conditions of people around the world.

I must emphasize that U.S. engineering firms that are engaged in the international market are holding their own based on quality, expertise and their commitment to the engineering profession. We are not being beaten by our competition in technology or program management skills. In fact, U.S. technical skills are highly sought after. However, when our competitors bring the full support of their government through tied aid trust funds into the picture, the rules of the game drastically change. **Foreign governments bring with them a sound understanding that their engineering industry is a vehicle for export promotion of their country's products and services.** Unlike our competition, my colleagues and I find we have few places in our own government to turn to thwart the challenges posed to us overseas. While the U.S. Government's support for the engineering industry has improved over the last ten years, we still need a commitment that matches our own in terms of not just staying competitive, but winning.

ACEC stands ready to support this committee, Congress and the Clinton Administration in their efforts to make U.S. business the engine of economic recovery.

I welcome any of your questions at this time.

○

EXAMINING THE CHILDREN'S GRADUATE MEDICAL EDUCATION PROGRAM

HEARING

BEFORE THE

SUBCOMMITTEE ON HEALTH

OF THE

COMMITTEE ON ENERGY AND COMMERCE
HOUSE OF REPRESENTATIVES

ONE HUNDRED NINTH CONGRESS

SECOND SESSION

MAY 9, 2006

Serial No. 109-87

Printed for the use of the Committee on Energy and Commerce

Available via the World Wide Web: http://www.access.gpo.gov/congress/house

U.S. GOVERNMENT PRINTING OFFICE

28-657PDF WASHINGTON : 2006

For sale by the Superintendent of Documents, U.S. Government Printing Office
Internet: bookstore.gpo.gov Phone: toll free (866) 512-1800; DC area (202) 512-1800
Fax: (202) 512-2250 Mail: Stop SSOP, Washington, DC 20402-0001

COMMITTEE ON ENERGY AND COMMERCE

JOE BARTON, Texas, *Chairman*

RALPH M. HALL, Texas
MICHAEL BILIRAKIS, Florida
Vice Chairman
FRED UPTON, Michigan
CLIFF STEARNS, Florida
PAUL E. GILLMOR, Ohio
NATHAN DEAL, Georgia
ED WHITFIELD, Kentucky
CHARLIE NORWOOD, Georgia
BARBARA CUBIN, Wyoming
JOHN SHIMKUS, Illinois
HEATHER WILSON, New Mexico
JOHN B. SHADEGG, Arizona
CHARLES W. "CHIP" PICKERING, Mississippi
Vice Chairman
VITO FOSSELLA, New York
ROY BLUNT, Missouri
STEVE BUYER, Indiana
GEORGE RADANOVICH, California
CHARLES F. BASS, New Hampshire
JOSEPH R. PITTS, Pennsylvania
MARY BONO, California
GREG WALDEN, Oregon
LEE TERRY, Nebraska
MIKE FERGUSON, New Jersey
MIKE ROGERS, Michigan
C.L. "BUTCH" OTTER, Idaho
SUE MYRICK, North Carolina
JOHN SULLIVAN, Oklahoma
TIM MURPHY, Pennsylvania
MICHAEL C. BURGESS, Texas
MARSHA BLACKBURN, Tennessee

JOHN D. DINGELL, Michigan
Ranking Member
HENRY A. WAXMAN, California
EDWARD J. MARKEY, Massachusetts
RICK BOUCHER, Virginia
EDOLPHUS TOWNS, New York
FRANK PALLONE, JR., New Jersey
SHERROD BROWN, Ohio
BART GORDON, Tennessee
BOBBY L. RUSH, Illinois
ANNA G. ESHOO, California
BART STUPAK, Michigan
ELIOT L. ENGEL, New York
ALBERT R. WYNN, Maryland
GENE GREEN, Texas
TED STRICKLAND, Ohio
DIANA DEGETTE, Colorado
LOIS CAPPS, California
MIKE DOYLE, Pennsylvania
TOM ALLEN, Maine
JIM DAVIS, Florida
JAN SCHAKOWSKY, Illinois
HILDA L. SOLIS, California
CHARLES A. GONZALEZ, Texas
JAY INSLEE, Washington
TAMMY BALDWIN, Wisconsin
MIKE ROSS, Arkansas

BUD ALBRIGHT, *Staff Director*
DAVID CAVICKE, *General Counsel*
REID P. F. STUNTZ, *Minority Staff Director and Chief Counsel*

SUBCOMMITTEE ON HEALTH

NATHAN DEAL, Georgia, *Chairman*

RALPH M. HALL, Texas
MICHAEL BILIRAKIS, Florida
FRED UPTON, Michigan
PAUL E. GILLMOR, Ohio
CHARLIE NORWOOD, Georgia
BARBARA CUBIN, Wyoming
JOHN SHIMKUS, Illinois
JOHN B. SHADEGG, Arizona
CHARLES W. "CHIP" PICKERING, Mississippi
STEVE BUYER, Indiana
JOSEPH R. PITTS, Pennsylvania
MARY BONO, California
MIKE FERGUSON, New Jersey
MIKE ROGERS, Michigan
SUE MYRICK, North Carolina
MICHAEL C. BURGESS, Texas
JOE BARTON, Texas
(EX OFFICIO)

SHERROD BROWN, Ohio
Ranking Member
HENRY A. WAXMAN, California
EDOLPHUS TOWNS, New York
FRANK PALLONE, JR., New Jersey
BART GORDON, Tennessee
BOBBY L. RUSH, Illinois
ANNA G. ESHOO, California
GENE GREEN, Texas
TED STRICKLAND, Ohio
DIANA DEGETTE, Colorado
LOIS CAPPS, California
TOM ALLEN, Maine
JIM DAVIS, Florida
TAMMY BALDWIN, Wisconsin
JOHN D. DINGELL, Michigan
(EX OFFICIO)